THE AUTHOR

Dr. Keshav M. Mutalik retired as Principal, Sydenham College of Commerce and Economics, then worked as Hon. Director of the Sydenham Institute of Management and Entrepreneurial Studies, which he started. Later, he was Director of the Maharashtra Government's Central Services Training Institute, Bombay. He earned a Ph. D degree from the University of Bombay for his work on *Francis William Bain* and another Ph. D degree awarded by the Leeds University (U.K.) for his "A Socio-Linguistic Study of Kannada." Dr. Mutalik has established himself as a distinguished teacher, researcher and a connoisseur of drama and music. At present, he teaches Communication Skills and Research Methodology in The Mozambique-Tanzania Centre for Foreign Relations, Dar es Salaam, Tanzania, where he is Associate Professor.

Dr. Mutalik visited the U.S.A. as a senior Fulbright scholar where he studied Mark Twain's Visit to India and produced Indian plays in translation. His study on Mark Twain is published under the title *Mark Twain in India.*

Of late, Dr. Mutalik has undertaken an intensive study of Madhva Philosophy (Madhva Siddhanta) and has published books, *Guru Raghuvendra Swamy, Jagannath Dasa, Shri Raghoottma Teertha, Songs of Divinity,* and *Harikathamrutasara, A Few Pillars of Madhva Siddhanta.* His study of Vyasaraya Teertha, Vadiraja Teertha and Guru Madhva are awaiting publication.

JAGANNATH DASA'S

HARIKATHAMRUTASARA

(Quintessence of Hari's Saga)

Translated from Kannada
by
KESHAV M. MUTALIK

FOCUS

POPULAR PRAKASHAN
BOMBAY

POPULAR PRAKASHAN PVT LIMITED
35-C, Pandit Madan Mohan Malaviya Marg
Popular Press Bldg., Opp. 'Roche'
Tardeo, Bombay 400 034

First published 1995

(4048)

ISBN 81-7154-787-7

PRINTED IN INDIA

By Siddhi Offset Pvt Ltd., 5/12, Kamath Industrial Estate,
396, Veer Savarkar Marg, Prabhadevi,
Bombay-400 025.

HARIKATHAMRUTASARA
(in English Translation)

is respectfully dedicated to
His Holiness Shri Vibudhesha Teertha Swamiji
of
Admar Math, Udupi

CONTENTS

INTRODUCTION

Thirteen years today the author's beloved wife, Kumud, suddenly breathed her last despite the medical aid and Lord's prayers. The author became a rudderless boat groping in the vast waters of the world. With an innocent son, the only earthly support and hope, the author spent days and days, dazed, horrified and completely defeated. His sustaining activities were his job that kept him fairly busy and the hope of his son's future. Days rolled on, weeks turned into months, months to years and years into a decade. The mystery of life has not yet - in fact never - been understood except by seers. "Wasn't there in God's huge world a small place for my wife?" I used to think. But who, except He alone, can listen to the soulful cries? Tears rolled down several times, dried by cold breeze, washed by more tears. Nothing will bring back the dead wife, the mother for my son, the unseen mother-in-law for my daughter-in-law and the unseen grandmother for my grand-children. My grand-daughter very innocently, but philosophically, asked me today morning, "Dada (that's what they call me by) why don't you cry today?" Indeed "Yes". What tears will bring back solace to a broken heart? I didn't answer. Jocularly I told her to cry. The child's innocence has meaning. Tears do make one's sorrow light. But the author's sorrow is heavier than a mountain, and indelible like fast colour. He remembered the best way to "cry" - to write something great to the sacred memory of the dead. Here's what he has done.

Having soaked himself in the astounding life-story of Jagannath Dasa, the author considers it his bounden duty to translate Jagannath Dasa's *magnum opus*, *Harikathamrutasara* into English. To understand *Harikathamrutasara*, its beauty and poetic and literary grace itself is an achievement bestowed upon the reader by God; to translate it into English, a language that is culturally, philosophically different is indeed a laudable exercise almost verging on foolhardiness. Guru Madhva's *Dvaita* philosophy has been explained, re-explained, simplified and exemplified by a host of very able and illustrious scholars ranging from the redoubtable Jayatirth, Vyasatirth and Raghavendratirth to many others. Still Pandits scratch their brains to comprehend many propositions, illustrations and explanations. The very philosophy passes beyond a common man's powers of understanding. To realise it in Jagannath's *Harikathamrutasara* requires a high standard of mental and moral capacities. Is it not, therefore, the height of ignorance to translate it into English for readers to enjoy the beauties of the great Dasa's poem? Is not the author trying to do the impossible in his life? The only consolation is, perhaps, Jagannath Dasa may have given the author a major portion of his grace, scholarship and knowledge. This may have prompted the author to undertake the stupendous task of translating the poem into English. The author in all humility, accepts the fact - (If the Lord wills, what is impossible to achieve?).

At the height of his glory Jagannath Dasa visited Mysore and was honoured by the Court. This happened at the fag end of his career. Jagannath Dasa then settled at Manavi and did not undertake further journeys. He devoted a major portion of his time to writing. It is strongly believed that during this period the Dasa one day had a dream in which Shripadaraja, Vyasaraya, Vadiraja, and Purandara Das appeared and advised him to undertake the writing of a book on the Dvaita philosophy. "Write in Kannada a book that would, like Shrimun Nyaya Sudha of Jayatirth, explain the intricate philosophy of the great Madhvacharya," said the saints to Jagannath Dasa. "You are capable of doing it and must accomplish it," they said. The orders of the dream were accepted and Jagannath Dasa prayed to the Lord to give him intellectual and physical strength to complete the work. In his humility he has said in *Harikathamrutasara* "I am writing this story of Lord Hari with the kindness and grace of my Gurus". The work, ordered by the Gurus was commenced immediately and was entitled *Harikathamrutasara*, the essence of the nectar of the story of Hari.

The first part of *Harikathamrutasara* (Harikatha for short) was started at Manavi when Jagannath Dasa was nearly eighty years old. Though old and physically weak the Dasa started writing, the *magnum opus*, *Harikatha*. It is said that his hands used to tremble, his eyebrows, now become loose, expanded skin were covering his eyes, the entire body was emaciated. The Dasa's disciples used to lift the loose skin of the eyebrow and the trembling hand was steadied. "Why, Sir, are you writing in this condition?" asked Jagannath Dasa's disciples. "Why don't you rest? You are eighty. You have already done your work," they continued. Jagannath Dasa smiled at the disciples. Most lovingly he said: "Dear disciples, do you think I am writing this? It is the Lord because of His desire to spread the knowledge of His creation and because He wants to bless all souls, has been Himself writing through me. The Lord is putting the words in my mind and moving my hands to write. I have to obey Shri Hari's dictates." The words satisfied the disciples. The Dasa wrote the great work to propagate Dvaita Siddhanta and the greatness of God. *Harikathamrutasara* is recited in every house and is listened to with reverence.

It is strongly believed that after the first part of *Harikatha* was written, Jagannath Dasa moved to a village named Konanatambige in Haveri Taluka of Dharwad district. The village is on the bank of the river Varada. It is a smallish island, a place very good for serious writing activity. It was here at that time the pontiffs of Raghavendra Swami Mutt Shri Dhirendratirth and of Uttaradi Mutt Shri Satyabodhatirth spent their time and used to invite Jagannath Dasa for philosophic discussions. On the island was written *Harikatha* in thirtytwo cantos - and containing 988 stanzas. The work was ready except for the traditional benedictory canto. The Dasa was about to write the final canto when again he had a dream in which the Gurus prohibited him from writing the benedictory canto. "Don't you do it. It is reserved for your disciple. Find him out," thundered the voice in the dream. But where to find a disciple? What clues had he? These thoughts tormented Jagannath Dasa.

Jagannath Dasa spent sleepless nights to find out that disciple. Finally he decided to go to Karajagi near Haveri. Karajagi then was a seat of great learning and a home of Dvaita scholars. It was here that Jagannath Dasa decided to find his disciple. He held a number of meetings on philosophy; at the end of each discussion he would pose questions. "The one who answered correctly," he thought "was the right disciple." Many meetings were held, many great scholars attended them; but not one could answer Jagannath Dasa's questions. After several disappointments and near defeats, the Dasa addressed his last meeting. Questions were asked. No one answered. But as the Dasa was about to throw his hands up in despair, one Dasappa, an uncouth rustic stood up to answer. Though a Brahmin, Dasappa was just an apology for Brahmin culture, tradition and dress. It was the first time that he attended Jagannath Dasa's discourses and that because his good, pious wife had begged of him. Dasappa had his mouth full with betel-leaves and tobacco with the red saliva streaking down his mouth-sides. He would wipe it with the end of his *dhotee*. The moment of realization in Dasappa's life had come. He answered the Dasa's questions correctly and astounded everyone in the gathering. Jagannath Dasa could not contain his happiness and a little surprise. “What on earth is this?” he said, “You Dasappa, a burning flame of knowledge is so strangely hidden by your dirty dress and dirtier habits. Why should this be so?” Dasappa had his shock and self-realisation. He fell at Jagannath Dasa’s feet and bewailed, “Swami, bless this wretched person. I am your slave. I am your Dasa.” Jagannath Dasa blessed him and gave him the signet name, “Shrida Vitthal”. He is also called Karajagi Dasa. Dasappa became a great Dasa and wrote a number of songs. It was he who wrote the benedictory canto which is the thirtythird in the poem. The Harikatha was thus completed.

The present author has, in translating the poem, undertaken the heavy responsibility of climbing Mt Everest without any aid and single-handed. He has done it out of love and reverence to the great Jagannath Dasa. In his effort he was most enthusiastically supported by his son, Venkatesh, and his dear friend Dr Muttagi. Both of them (very earnestly but a little over-admiringly of the author’s talents) dissuaded the author from translating only a couple of stanzas. Their trust would be misplaced without the blessings of the author’s Gurus and Swamis.

One of the Swamis - a living example of Dvaita Siddanta and all it stands for - is Poojya Vibudhesha Teertha Swamiji of Admar Mutt, Udupi. The Swamiji’s love and kindly courtesy for all is proverbial. The author is proud to be a donee of a large measure of the Swamiji’s blessings. It was the Swamiji who readily agreed to honour my book on Jagannath Dasa (His Life and Works) by his Note of Blessings. It was the Swamiji who taught me the value of values in life. I am most grateful to him. As a token of my reverence I dedicate this book to the Poojya Swamiji.

Dar es Salaam, Keshav Mutalik
Tanzania.
Friday, 16 November 1990.

THE GENERAL PLAN AND BEAUTY OF HARIKATHAMRUTASARA

It has to be indisputably accepted that the greatest contribution of Jagannath Dasa to literature and philosophic thought is his *Harikatha* which may rightly be considered to be a Dvaita Bible. It is the quintessence of Dvaita philosophy and a definitive book on Madhva Sinddhanta. A student who wants to understand, master and propagate Madhva Siddhanta has necessarily to read the book because being in Kannada, *Harikatha* explains the subtle intricacies of the Siddhanta. It is the *Summum Bonum* for all Dvaitins.

That such a great writing fructified when Jagannath Dasa was eighty and that he, with sustained efforts, could write thirtytwo cantos is a marvel of devotion and the blessings of God. The Dasa an old man with dim light in his eyes and trembling hand, sat up with a pillar to support his back. The pillar is still maintained as a mark of respect for the Dasa. Only intense devotion and emotional mingling of the individual soul with the Godhead as a servant made the Dasa and other disciples work totally ignoring physical discomfort. It was such devotion that prompted the sculptors to carve temples; it was this devotion that brought painters to execute marvellous art, Jagannath Dasa sat for hours writing *Harikatha* as a worship of Shri Hari. The book is not only a religious manifesto but also an excellent piece of poetry.

The *magnum opus* of *Harikatha* runs into thirtytwo cantos with one final benedictory canto added by Shrida Vitthal, Karajgi Dasappa. Dasappa became Jagannath Dasa's ardent disciple and was considered to be the only person fit to write the concluding canto. This canto, known as "Phala Shruti Sandhi" (a canto that declares blessings on the reader) describes the many earthly pleasures and benefits that one gets by reading an intensely religious book like Harikatha. In a lavishly flattering style Dasappa has pointed out how the poem is a quintessence, a gist of Dvaita Siddanta. The first thirtytwo cantos are composed by Jagannath Dasa.

One has to understand a brief summary of all the cantos before going deeper into each canto and its interpretation. The original manuscript completed by Jagannath Dasa is not available. It may have been lost or kept by someone. So far it has not appeared on the scene for scholars and disciples to study. Many publishers of the so-called *Harikatha* have published it dividing the text into different cantos and sections. They have done it indiscriminately and unsystematically. In a situation like this it is difficult to prove the authenticity or otherwise of the publishers' actions. Many scholars, however, accept the authoritativeness of the work with commentary prepared by Shri Sankarshana Wodeyar and of the commentary of *Bhava Prakash*, (edited by Padmanabh Dasa). The present translation is based on the edition prepared by Kalamdani Gururaya (Shri Harikathamrutasara : edited by Kalamdani Gururaya : Published by A.M. Karadi and Sons, Hubli: 1982, price Rs.15.00).

There have been many commentaries on Harikatha in Telugu, Kannada and Sanskrit. Even the Kannada commentary was written in Telugu script. The chief commentaries in Kannada are by:

1. Shri Sankarshana Wodeyar's commentary written in Telugu script.
2. (Modkal Shesharao) Guru Vijaya Vitthal.
3. (Kuntoji Dasa) Guru Shrisha Vitthal.
4. Draupadesh Vitthal.
5. (Jamakhandi Vadirajacharya) Bhavasoochana Comentary.
6. Padmanabha Dasa's *Bhava Prakashike.*
7. Harikathamrutasara edited by Kalamdani Gururaya.

The Sanskrit commentaries are by Jamakhandi Vadirajacharya (Shri Vyasadasha-Siddhanta Kaumudi) and anonymous writing named Tamrapaniya. Many disciples believed that Jagannath Dasa was Salhada, brother of Pralhada, in his previous birth. The thirty-two cantos are given titles to indicate the subject-matter.

Canto One : The first canto called "Mangalacharana", invocation to God, invokes the blessings of gods, saints and gurus in achieving the successful completion of the poem. The other cantos are

Canto Two : Karuna Sandhi (Canto of Compasssion) where the author (poet) seeks the compassion of the most benevolent god.

Canto Three : Vyapati Sandhi (Canto of Omnipresence) points out the immense world of the creator and how He is found present all over His creation. He is omnipresent.

Canto Four : Bhojana Rasa Vibhaga Sandhi (Canto of the division of essences in food) refers to God's sentiments as compared with the essences of food. The devotee has to seek God's love.

Canto Five : Vibhooti Sandhi (Canto of Divinity in Creation) explains the presence of the Lord in different aspects of His creation. He lives in Shaligram (black round pebbeles found in Gandak river in North India), Tulasi (basil plant) and in the heavenly bodies.

Canto Six : Pancha Maha Yajna Sandhi (Canto of five great fire sacrifices) mentions the fire, a vehicle of sacrifice, in various forms in the world.

Canto Seven : Pancha Tanmatra Sandhi (Canto of five senses) deals with watching inside through knowledge and practising penance.

Canto Eight : Matruka Sandhi (Canto of meditation using all parts of the body) refers to involving all parts of the body to meditate on the Lord.

Canto Nine : Jeevaprakarana Sandhi or Udatta Anudatta Sandhi (Canto of the existence of God) mentions the greatness of Shri Hari and how a devotee can understand Him.

Canto Ten : Sarva Prateeka Sandhi (Canto of God's presence) explains God's presence everywhere.

Canto Eleven : Dhyana Prakriya. Sandhi or Sthavara Jangama Sandhi (Canto of paths of meditation or the living and the non-living) mentions the forms of worship and discusses the living and the non-living.

Canto Twelve : Nadee Prakarana Sandhi (Canto of Many Veins) delineates the different muscular parts and the veins of the body and the manifestation of the divine presence in each small part of the body. The Lord receives the devotee's worship in all forms of the body.

Canto Thirteen : Namasmarana Sandhi (Canto of Lord's prayer) is devoted to the prayers of God and the protection that the Lord gives for the devotion. One has to utter prayers while sleeping, while doing one's work and dedicate the entire time and body to the Lord.

Cantos Fourteen and Fifteen : Pitrugana Sandhi (Canto of ancestors) indicates the worship of God through one's offering of food to ancestors. The food offered to many ancestors reaches them in many ways. Shwasa Sandhi (Canto of breath) continues the discussion in the area of breathing and through it god-realization.

Cantos Sixteen and Seventeen : Datta Swatantrya Sandhi (Canto of offered freedom) and Svagata Swatantrya Sandhi (Canto of inner freedom) explain how man's action is the result of Shri Hari's good wishes. Man depends entirely on the Lord's grace. The dasa points out the free action of God in relation to man's dependence on the creator.

Canto Eighteen : Sarva Swatantrya Sandhi or Krida Vilas Sandhi (Canto of total freedom or Canto of joyful play) relates to the complete independence of the Lord. Without Him the world cannot move. Each creation of God works according to the Lord's orders.

Canto Nineteen : Karma Vimochana Sandhi (Canto of release from action) points to the duties of man, how he should perform them and how he would be relieved of the duties. If man remembers Shri Hari and performs the duties enjoined on him, then man is free from the bonds of duty.

Cantos Twenty and Twenty One : Gunataratamya Sandhi and Brahattaratamya Sandhi (Canto of Levels of Qualities and Canto of Levels of Larger and more expansive Qualities) explain the relationship that exists among the many creations of God. Jagannath Dasa, in an elaborate manner points out the many levels of attainment. In fact, the basic principle or Dvaita Philosophy is the *Taratamya Bhava,* levels of distinctions and the acceptance of hierarchy.

Canto Twenty Two : Sakaladuritanivarana Sandhi (Canto of release from all problems) is a prayer to God to remove all the worldly obstacles and to bless everyone with a life of dedication. Unqualified surrender to God is a path to God-realization.

Cantos Twenty Three, Twenty Four, Twenty Five, Twenty Six and *Twenty Seven* : Aparoksha Taratamya, Bimbapratibimba, Arohana Taratamya, Avarohana Taratamya, Anukramanika Taratamya - all Sandhis or Cantos describe the hierarchy or Taratamya (differentiation) or ranking among Lord's creation. These are according to Dvaita Siddhanta.

Canto Twentyeight : Vighneshwara Stotra Sandhi (Canto of Lord Ganapati's praise) prays to Ganapati for his blessings. In fact, this should have come as the first canto. But Jagannath Dasa inserts this in between the Taratamya cantos.

Cantos Twentynine and Thirty : Anutaratamya and Daitya Taratamya Sandhis (Cantos of Minute differentiation and of Difference in evil) once again relate to the principle of differentiation.

Canto Thirtyone : Naivedya Samarpana Sandhi (Canto of Offering) is an offering to God. The Dasa describes in great detail how one has to offer the devotion in the form of meditation, food and flowers.

Canto Thirtytwo : Kakshataratamya Sandhi (Canto of Divine Differentiation) again is a prayer to Gods. This the last canto and repeats the supremacy of Shri Hari. Laxmi, Vayu and all other gods have also been invoked for blessings.

Canto Thirtythree : Phalashruti Sandhi (Canto of Benediction) as already mentioned, was composed by Karajagi Dasa or Dasappa. It speaks of the blessings of the Lord on those who read and recite the poem Harikatha. The reading and recitation must not be mechanical but must be by fully concentrating on God.

Harikathamrutasara is a grand poem extending to thirtytwo cantos and is written in a highly literary style. Jagannath Dasa, like Milton, wants to emphasize the ways of God to man. Madhvacharya's Dvaita philosophy was explained to the people in many writings by Sanyasis and attracted studies and researches. Jayateerth, Vyasaraya, and Raghvendra Swamy, wrote many commentaries. Dvaita philosophy was carried to the common man in Kannada by the Dasas such as Purandara Dasa, Vijaya Dasa and Gopala Dasa. But no one actually immersed himself in Sanskrit studies to understand the subtleties of philosophy and then to explain them in literary Kannada. The purpose of the earlier Dasas was to spread Dvaita to the layman. But by now the layman was educated and wanted to learn more about Dvaita. Additionally, the Dasas, because of their scant training in Sanskrit, were not respected by Pandits. It was Jagannath Dasa who alone could bridge the gulf between Sanskrit learning and Kannada writing for the benefit of the common man.

The plan of the cantos indicates the wide range of the Dasa's study and covers every aspect of Madhva philosophy. The poem is written in "Bhamini Shatpadi" and is well-suited for musical rendering. Of significance is Jagannath Dasa's constant references to arithemetic figures like "Arumuredondu Savira" (six, three, two and one thousand = twentyone, 6 x 3 = 18, + 2 + 1) to exactly indicate the number of years of penance of parts of the body, of creations of God - to quantify the statements. Similarly, the hierarchy in the Lord's creation is so well defined that the reader clearly understands the level of differences.

Harikatha poetizes "Bhakti" (devotion, surrender to God) in a lucid manner. A devotee must understand that he cannot realize the presence of God unless he surrenders himself to the Lord. In the seventeenth stanza of the tenth canto the Dasa says -

Enu kelidarenu Nodida /
Renu Odidarenu Pelida /
Renu Padidarenu Madidarenu Dinadinadi //
Shrinivasana Janmakarma Sa /
Danuragadi Nenedu Tatt /
Tsthanadali Tadrupa Tannamakana Smarisadava //

(What use is it if one read, heard or studied? Unless one immerses oneself in Shri Hari's meditation, nothing is achieved.)

God is all-pervasive yet mysteriously unknown. He is there; yet not there. Fire exists inwardly, latently in wood, coal and any combustible matter. But that fire does not present itself outwardly. In a beautiful account Jagannath Dasa writes -

Parimalavu Sumandadol Analanu /
Araniyola gippante Damo /
Daranu Bramhadigala Manadali Tori Toradale //
Irutiha Jagannath Vithalana /
Karuna Padeva Mumukshu Veevaru /
Parama Bhagavataranu Kondadaduvudu Pratidinavu //
(Canto I Stanza 13)

(Like fragrance in flower, like fire in wood, Lord Damodara lives as if not present in all His creations. So, those who aspire for salvation should worship Jagannath Vitthala.)

That God is omnipresent and manifests Himself everywhere provided the devotee has a humble approach is stressed in many stanzas.

Obbanali Nintaduvunu Ma
Ttobbanali Noduvanu Beduva
Nobbanali Needuvanu Mataduvanu Beragagi
(Canto II Stanza 9)

(He, Shri Hari, plays in the form of one, He sees through the second one, He asks through the third and looks surprised through another.)

The idea of the Lord's existence in His creation is emphasized in the Geeta. Jagannath Dasa mentions the concept of omniscience and omnipresence in a major part of *Harikatha*.

Jagannath Dasa does not believe in rituals and false devotionless worship. In fact, these ideas have been expressed by all saints and Dasas. It is absolutely futile to fall at the feet of the Lord and to utter prayers without devotion.

The Dasa says:

Snana Japa Devarchaneyu Vya
Khyan Bharata Muhop Pu
Rana Kathegala Pelidarenu Dinadinadi /
Jnyana Karmendriya Galinde /
Nenu Maduva Karmagalu Laku /
Meenivasan Poojeyandarpisada Manavanu //
(Canto XIII Stanza 6)

(What is the good of a bath, reading of the Lord's story, and a lecture on the books? If the action performed is not dedicated to the Lord (Laxmi Nivas) it is totally useless.)

The *Harikatha* stresses the need to totally surrender oneself to Shri

Hari. The Lord should be remembered all the twentyfour hours of the day. He should be prayed when asleep and when awake. The entire scheme of man should be oriented to the Lord's service and remembrance. In return the Lord takes care of the devotee. He becomes the servant of servants to protect the devotee.

Makkaladisuvaga Madadiyo /
Lakkaradi Nalivaga Haya Pa /
Llakki Gaja Modalada Vahanagaleri Mere Vaga //
Bikkuvaga Akalisutali De /
Vakkitanayana Nenewutiha Nara /
Sikkanu Yamadootarige Avavalli Nodidaru //
(Canto XIII Stanza 1)

(When one is playing with children, when sweetly talking to his wife, while riding a horse or a palanquin, while yawning or hiccupping, if the devotee remembers Lord Krishna, the God of Death (Yama) will find it difficult to search him.)

Jagannath Dasa justifies even simple or casual devotion to Lord Shri Hari. The smallest worship is bound to reward the devotee with the largest dividend. In this regard God has no preferences or prejudices. Irrespective of the devotee's status the Lord blesses him with favours.

Avakuladava Nadareni /
Nyava Deshadoriddareni /
Nyava Karmava Madaleninyava Kaladali //
Shri Varana Sarvatradali Sam /
Bhavisuta Poojisuta Modipa /
Kovidaringunteno Bhayaduhkadi Dwandwagalu //
(Canto XIII, Stanza 4)

(Let him belong to any caste, let him come from any country, let him follow any profession, if he worships Shrinivasa, He will accept him.)

God is benevolent, merciful and understanding. He is interested in bringing to His devotees the maximum amount of happiness and solace. The devotee has to acknowledge the supremacy of the Lord. So, Jagannath Dasa enjoins on all human beings to worship the Lord to obtain His blessings. "Worship the image of Shri Hari," he says. Of course, to attain the worshipping state of mind, one has to give up greed, selfishness and ego. The Dasa says :

Oratubuddhiya Bidu Laukika /
Harategala Needadi Kanchana /
Paratiloshtadigalu Samavendaritu Nityadali //
(Canto XIV Stanza 16)

(Give up arrogance and talks of worldly benefits. Shun your greed for gold, wealth and power.)

The ego is nothing but a misjudged bravado. "It is" says the Dasa, "like fighting a battle with a needle." (Sooji Karadali Pididu Samarava Na Jayisuvenu Emba Naranante.)

Speaking about the humility of the Lord for the benefit of His devotee, the Dasa says :

Malagi Paramadaradi Padalu /
Kulitu Keluva Kultitu Padalu /
Niluva Nintalze Naliva Nalidare Olive Nimagemba //
Sulabhano Hari Tannavara Nara /
Ghalige Bittagalanu Ramadhava /
Nolisaluriyade Pamararu Balaluvaru Bhavadolage //
(Canto II Stanza 5)

(If the devotee sleeps and worships, the Lords sits to listen to him; He will stand up when the devotee sits; if the devotee stands He will dance and sing. It is very easy to obtain the grace of Shri Hari.)

There are a number of examples of the the justification of the all-pervasiveness of the Lord. Man has to understand the divinity and the greatness of God. Jagannath Dasa has taken upon himself the onerous responsibility of praising the Lord and of explaining the supremacy of the Dvaita philosophy. In the epilogue the Dasa of Karajagi has succintly summarised the importance of *Harikatha*. He says :

Sakhendare Harikathamruta /
Sakhembuvudemma Guruvara /
Saridalladale Tiliyendenuta Mahendranandananu //
Sarathiya Balagondu Sara /
Saragala Nirnaisi Peladana /
Sara Nadeva Mahatmarige Samsara Vellihudo //
(Canto XXXIII Stanza 3)

(This is the essence of the religious principles. This is a praise of the charioteer of Arjuna.)

Jagannath Dasa's poem celestial encompasses the great Indian philosophic writings of the Vedas, the Upanishads and the Geeta. The principles of man-god relationship enunciated in Bramha Sutra are also lucidly explained. Dvaita Tatva (principles) was firmly established by Madhvacharya, the doyen of Dvaita Siddhanta. Jagannath Dasa in his *Harikatha* repeatedly states that Shri Hari is not easily "seeable," is beyond the reach of even the greatest Yogis. Yet by sheer piety, self-surrender and devotion, He can be "seen" and His blessings cherished.

The poem as pointed out by Dasappa (Karajagi Dasa), contains the beauties of religion, philosophy and literature. There are the nine Rasas :

Harikathamrutasara Navarasa /
Bharita Bahugambhira Ratna /
Kara Ruchira Shrungara Salankara Vistara //
Sarasa Narakanthiravacha /
Yara Janita Sukumara Satvi /
Karige Paramodara Modida Mare Yadupakara //
(Canto XXXIII Stanza 14)

(Harikatha contains the nine Rasas and is tastefully extensive like the sea. Jagannath Dasa, by offering this poem, has rendered an unredeemable service to people.)

The greatness of the poem lies in stressing again and again the fact that Lord Shri Hari is obtainable by all. No sect, no past vices and sins, no ignorance, no great learning will prevent a devotee from reaching God and making his life awakened, refined and holy.

Dushtarennade Durvishayadin /
Pushtarennade Pootakarma /
Bharashtarennade Shri Da Vitthal Venu Gopala //
Krishna Kaipidiyuvanu Satya Vi /
Sishtadasatvanu Palisi /
Nishteyindali Harikathamrutasara Pathisuvara //
(Canto XXXIII Stanza 24)

(The Lord does not discriminate against the wicked, the people deep in worldly luxuries, the sinful and the fallen; He will hold His helping hand to lift the people that read *Harikathamrutasara* with love, respect and devotion.)

Many are the beauties of the poem. Jagannath Dasa has rendered a great service to people by writing a literary philosophic compendium in *Harikatha.* The more one reads it, the more one redeems oneself from vice, avarice and ignorance, *Harikatha* is indeed Jagannath Dasa's swan song.

AUTHOR'S NOTE ON TRANSLATION

The author has many times mentioned in the Introduction the problem of translating *Harikatha* into English. Jagannath Dasa is a great Pandit; his Kannada is highly Sanskritised and literary. To understand *Harikatha* is by itself a Herculean task; to attempt to translate it into a foreign language like English is almost achieving the impossible. It is *tour de force* testing the author's competence and devotion.

The author has translated the poem into free verse which many times is a euphemism for prose. He has tried to make his translation enjoyable. The credit will certainly go to Jagannath Dasa if he (author) has succedded in making the translation delightful. Any failure in that regard should wholly and squarely be placed on the author and his foolish endeavour. He has exposed his ignorance and incompetence.

To assist the reader in understanding some areas of the poem the author has given notes. These explain the points of poetry and philosophy. As far as possible the author has seen to it that he has not loaded the poem with his own reading of the poem. He honestly feels that a rose should be left to itself to crow about its beauty and fragrance; the author should not poke his unclean nose to contaminate it. The poem shows its beauty, literary excellences and grace. Any uncalled for comments spoil its architectural grandeur and make it look a common steel and cement concrete building. Here, the author as a commentator should announce the scores of the game and not how the game has been played, how it should have been played or how it will be played. Guru Madhva and the Dasas like Jagannath Dasa are seers extraordinaire; they are not cheap philosophers and poets who want to cash their knowledge at the altar of a publisher. They, therefore, need no advertisement, no unwanted commentary. The translation is done to make the Kannada poem understood by non-Kannada readers. With the sweetness and light of the translation, if any, the reader is urged to go to the original poem - if not the entire poem at least a major part of it. That would bring the blessings of *Harikatha* on the reader and the translator.

Canto I

INVOCATION

(It is customary to begin any work, undertaking and writing with an invocation to Gods who are expected to remove all obstacles in the work and bless its successful completion. Jagannath Dasa offers humble prayers to Shri Hari whose story he has undertaken to narrate, His spouse Rama or Laxmi, Bramha, the Creator and all other gods and goddesses and the Gurus and preceptors.)

All Lord's devotees listen to with respect
Hari's nectar-like saga I've recited
With preceptors' blessings.

(Jagannath Dasa is believed to have worshipped Narasimha - half human half lion god - who is his personal favourite God. Each saint, each Guru or Dasa has his own personal God whom he worships as an incarnation of Lord Vishnu. Aside from Moola Rama always ritually worshipped by all the Dvaita Sanyasis, many of them have Venu Gopala, Hayavadana as their chosen Gods. The Sanyasis are always shown in imaginary pictures and paintings to be worshipping their chosen Lord. It must be noted that the chosen God is ultimately Vishnu.)

I salute Narasimha who kindly showers auspiciousness.
Worshipped by the lotus hands of Rama;
His charming feet are reverentially adored
By Bramha, Saraswati, Vayu, Bharati, Garuda, Shesha, Indra.
Who's cause of world's creation, stability and destruction. (1)

(After saluting Vishnu following the order of precedence Jagannath Dasa salutes Hari's consort, Laxmi, Goddesss of Wealth. When the ocean was churned by gods and demons to obtain life-sustaining nectar, Vishnu became a tortoise to hold the sinking mountain, Mandara. Mandara served as a churning rod. When the ocean was churned Laxmi came up from it and was married to Vishnu.)

Laxmi comprehends meticulously many qualities of the One
Who has world in belly; praises Him
For ventures unmentioned in Vedas and Puranas;
Joyous in Lord's prowess galore and proud

Of qualities three.
Laxmi, great Goddess, my salutation to you. (2)

(Next to Vishnu in order of precedence according to Madhva philosophy of differentiatiion (Taratamya Bhava) is Bramha, who has been entrusted by Vishnu the work of creation. Bramha married Saraswati, Goddess of knowledge, learning and speech. Bramha is worshipped by Gods lower in rank than himself. The author remembers him and meditates on him.)

Salutations to Bramha son of Shri Hari, a mass of
incomparable joy.
Bramha revered by other gods, pure and real
Is a Sun to Saraswati's Lotus face; father of Garuda, Shesha
and Rudra and a world preceptor.
Let him kindly bless me with pure powers of intellect. (3)

(Jagannath Dasa remembers Vayudeva (Wind God) who offers many blessings to mortals.

Let Guru Vayu protect us. He breathes into
Six Three Two and One thousand and
Twice three hundred recitals. Living myriads (of)
Years making mortals pray. Bestows
Solace to pure, good life to
Centrists and hell to the sinners. (4)

(It is customary to bow down to Saraswati, Goddess of Knowledge. She is the presiding deity of wisdom. She has the powers to grant every thing connected with learning and writing. Without her grace no intellectual activity can progress. Jagannath Dasa therefore salutes Saraswati.)

Bramha's wife, Saraswati, unlimited repository of knowledge,
Goddess proud of Vedas and holding a lute.
I salute you, Guru's wife. Staying
On my tongue grant me faculty to
Praise the Lord, Laxmi's consort. (5)

(In the next stanza, too, praise of the Goddess of Learning is continued.)

Daughter of Krutidevi and Pradyumna,
Wife of Maruti preceptor of gods who
Have mastered twentyfour principles, bless me
With unshaking devotion to Hari. Let me
Recollect the quintessence of Bhagawat and Bharat. (6)

(Vedavyasa is so called because he compiled the Vedas that have been the utterances of God. He has written the Mahabharat and has been considered to have authored Bhagawat. Vyasa is the supreme preacher and master of Vishnu's greatness and omnipresence. He is the teacher royal to other gods. He is indeed Lord Vishnu incarnate. All writers salute him to obtain his blessings.)

You have granted knowledge to Bramha, a receptacle of the
Vedas
To Indra and other gods. Breathing eternal joy,
You purify the world. Freed from vices,
Illnesses and baser thoughts you are
Worshipped by gods and are protector of the good.
You, Vedavyasa, save me from world's miseries. (7)

(In the next stanza the author narrates the reasons for Madhva's birth. Madhva or Anandatirtha, is accepted as an incarnation of Vayu or Maruti. The world was corrupted by false propaganda about religion. Spurious books on religion were written by Manimanta and others and were contributing to moral debasement. At that time, Bramha or Vayu, consort of Saraswati, was born in a small family and undertook to preach the genuine principles of philosophy.)

The world witnessed twentyone corrupt commentaries
Popularised by Manimanta and other sinners.
Then was born to Madhya Geha Bhatta
And his wife a world preacher Madhva,
Famous all over. I salute him, a Guru par excellence. (8)

(Jagannath Dasa refers, briefly, to Madhva's philosophical tenets. He mentions why people remember Madhva and reiterates his greatness.)

Lord Vishnu is Master of five differentiated world.
His servants are Bramha, Ridra, Indra, other gods.
Madhva preached twentyfive tenets and level differences
among gods.
I salute him, Anandtirth who is Bramha of today. (9)

(Shiva or Shankara comes next in the hierachy of salutations. He is considered to be Bramha's son and Parvati's husband. Shankara is a formidable terror to his enemies. Living most of the time in Kailas, Shiva offers blessings to his worhippers. The author invokes his blessings and kindness.)

Shiva, Vamadeva and Bramha's son,
Parvati's husband, is a terror to enemies.
With Ganga in his tuft of hair, elephant hide to cover,
He is chief God, a love-god destroyer and resident of Kailas.
Rudra has Sun, Moon and fire in eyes;

But grants devotees' desires. May he bestow auspicious
period ! (10)

(Vishnu or Hari is Supreme and is timeless spaceless and free from all actions. But other gods and demigods and His creations are time and action bound. They have their actions, duties and penances imposed on them. To obtain the Lord's grace they engage themselves, in severe personal privations and fastings. Shiva, as illustrated here, undertook long periods of penance and devotion. To reach a higher level in the hierarchy Shiva studied the Vedas, mastered the philosophical tenets and was initiated into severe discipline.)

Tiger-skin covered Shiva accepted Bramha discipleship
For forty long ages (periods);
Studied Vedas and Shastras, practised severe
Penance sitting on the bank of Kalpa Sea.
Thus you earned chiefdom of gods and
Narayan's grace and became Shesha serving
As mattress for the Lord. Bless us. (11)

(Jagannath Dasa then salutes the other lesser gods, sages, ancestors, fairies and his Gurus. Also, he remembers all the senior Dasas.)

I salute Indra, other gods and sages
Ancestors, fairies and ascetics such as
Padmanabhatirth and others. Single-minded
Do I bow down to Dasas who indeed
Are servants of Laxmi's husband.

(Shri Hari lives and does not apparently live in the world. His presence is understood not by all but only by the initiated and the fully realised. People that desire to obtain the Lord's blessings should dedicate themselves to the reading of his stories and superhuman activities.)

Like fragrance in flowers, like fire in pieces of wood,
He, the Lord, lives in the mind of Bramha, and other gods;
Seekers of Lord Jagannath Vithal's mercy
Should bow down humbly to all devotees of Vishnu. (13)

(Thus ends the First Canto which is an invocation to all devotees of the Lord. The auspicious atmosphere to narrate/write Lord's story has been sought by Hari's mercy and blessings. Jagannath Dasa like all devotees, tells people that nothing is achieved without Hari's kindness. All obstacles are removed by Hari's blessings and auspicious touch. Hari is omnipresent, omnipotent and omniscient. Nothing moves without His will. Therefore Jagannath Dasa praises the Gurus, ascetics, sages and, above all, Shri Hari to grant him and the readers the quiet period conducive to narrating and listening to the deeds of Lord's prowess and infinite mercy.)

Canto II

LORD THE MERCIFUL

(Shri Hari is indeed very kind and considerate. He is a slave of His devotees and stands to obey their orders. The devotees must be genuinely interested in Hari's prayers, meditation and should wholeheartedly surrender to Him. The second canto very vividly narrates God-devotee relationship and proclaims the former's supremacy and mercifulness. It is the devotee who may falter, not Hari.)

(The first half of the stanza, "All Lord's devotees listen to ... with preceptors' blessings" being a key-note is repeated in the beginning. It is thus repeated in all subsequent cantos.)

(Shri Hari's story is pleasant to the ear, has the power of fulfilling one's desires and brings mental consolation. All devotees usually listen to it with attention and respect.)

Hari story is music to ear;
Dispels worldly sorrows
Protects us here and there (the other world).
Offering all earthly pleasures.
All people (Brahmins) should carefully
Hear Laxmi's Consort's auspicious
Story that indeed is sacred. (1)

(Jagannath Dasa continues his recital by illustrating his arguments about Hari's sacredness and pointing out how greatly His sanctity spreads.)

Rainwater flowing on the road is unusable.
The same good for bath on joining a big river.
Like that this story written though in impure
Language* is after all Hari, father of Ganga's praise
Hence great as ocean.
Brahmins accept it as sacred. (2)

(* Note 1 : Sanskrit was considered to be divine and all works in Sanskrit were fit for scholars' attention. Kannada and other languages derived from Sanskrit were inferior because they are Prakruts. They are considered unfit for sacred literature. Jagannath Dasa himself believed so and suffered untold miseries before he became a Dasa.)

(The author mentions in many examples to prove that despite Shri Hari's closeness to Laxmi and other gods and goddesses the Lord listens to the cry of even an ordinary devotee. His heart extends to all and is at his devotee's call.)

Lord Vishnu incomparable in greatness
Has all superior qualities. Laxmi, devotedly
Proud of Vedic collections, meditates
Constantly on Him yet sees Him not.
But He is achieved by the few noble-hearted
That worship His feet. Who can extol the Lord's mercy? (3)

(Shri Hari is present everywhere but is not achieved or seen by mere words or songs. His presence and seemingly absence is realised by His ardent devotees.)

The supreme Lord is not visible in mind or words
Yet He follows those who constantly remember Him.
Inside His belly is hidden the world
Yet shows He like others to have been born.
Such a Lord, praised by Bhisma and
Rider of Garuda, is found to listen
To His devotees' songs staying in their
House with other gods. (4)

(The infinite kindness of Hari is indescribable. Hari is the slave of the slave of Vishnu. He is around him and is easy to please. Jagannath Dasa has brought out the merciful qualities of Shri Hari in excellently couched words that speak not only of Lord's greatness but also of the author's disarmingly simple yet appealing literary style. Even philosophy is made lucid and uncumbersome. It is for such gems of writing that *HariKatha* is rated high in the literary world.)

Sleep and respectfully sing of Hari
He sits to listen; sing sitting, He stands;
Stand, He enjoys and you enjoy singing,
He grants His kindnesses; easy to please
Rama's consort, Hari, leaves not even for a moment,
His people (devotees). Fools not knowing this
Suffer incalculably wallowing in the world. (5)

(Hari is known to grant blessings on His devotees. He keeps nothing in arrears. Like a prosperous banker He makes payments with no loss of time. But the devotee has to earn Hari's goodwill by total surrender. In the following stanzas Jagannath Dasa narrates how Shri Hari watches His creation.)

Staying in mind calls Himself the Mind;
Grants joys and sorrows relative to their merit to the three
Types (Satva, Rajas and Tamas) of people.
Surrender mind and He presents Himself.
Grants heavenly bliss to them who
Slave everyday in His service. (6)
He is pure blessings incarnate; He alone
Frees people of wordly miseries.
Accept His supremacy and be granted total release.
Otherwise doing sacrifices, charities and
Actions as one's duty will entitle
One to blessings according to merit
Like in Arjuna and Duryodhana. (7)

(In the following stanzas Jagannath Dasa enumerates Shri Hari's activities and greatness. They mention how He pervading the entire world protects good people.)

Through four-faced Bramha He creates the world;
Through Rudra He destroys His creation;
Yet He has no form, no limit; ever present everywhere.
He protects His devotees who call Him
A mass of eternal joy and myriad named Lord. (8)

Residing in one He plays; watches through another;
Offers through someone and speaks with wonder through the third;
Awesomely Supreme Lord Hari fears none
Listens to none; a master of the world
He seemingly suffers and makes others suffer. (9)

To the supplicating He is a wishfulfulling tree;
Ever merciful and benevolent;
Laxmi's husband is purest of the pure with
Sacred and auspicious. This friend
Of Arjuna runs to caller's and if devotionally
Addressed as incomparable, bliss incarnate,
Misery killer. (10)

(How does Shri Hari watch His devotees? How does He save them from destruction, frustration and disappointment? Jagannath Dasa comes here to express the incomprehensible Love of Hari. He does it in a masterful Way using simple common day experiences. Each illustration explains vividly Lord's unfaltering kindness. The writer's literary style is an outcome of no studied effort but a natural overflow of personal involvement. Jagannath Dasa is no mere writer; he is a seer, a dedicated soldier in the service of God.)

Like a mother suddenly appearing as though
From a dark room to pacify her crying child?
Embracing the laughing child and wiping the tears,
Madhusudan presents Himself to His devotees
To wash their sorrows and to protect them. (11)
He offered Himself to stand on a devotedly flung brick;[1]
Bestowed all worldly fortune to a poor Brahmin for a handful of beaten rice;[2]
Placed him protected in His belly, the one who profusely insulted;
Mercilessly hit by arrows though, He pardoned Bhishma; He is merciful[3] (12)

(Notes : 1. This refers to Pundalik of Pandharpur who was serving his parents and had no time when Hari appeared before him. He did not want to wake up his tired parents when they were fast asleep on his lap. Pundalik threw a brick for Hari to stand for while. There He stood and is now Vitthal of Pandarpur.

2. This refers to Sudam, a poor Brahmin friend of Krishna. The Brahmin at his wife's suggestion went to meet Krishna in Dwaraka and took, as a gift a handful of beaten rice. The Lord took it from the poor man, ate it with great pleasure and bestowed on him all worldly fortune.

3. In the Mahabharata war Krishna had declared that he would not use his weapons. He worked only a charioteer to Arjuna. But Bhishma, commanding the Kaurava army had vowed that he would force Krishna to use his disc. Arrows were mercilessly showed on Krishna and even Hanuman sitting on the chariot. In anger Krishna took out his disc to fight and broke his promise. Bhishma was pleased that the Lord fulfilled Bhishma's vow.)

A serpent that guards wealth not enjoying it itself
Nor passing it to others; yet happy with its duty.
Like that Laxmi's consort protects His devotees expecting nothing.
The ever-joyful, none-to-equal Lord accepts not wicked people's service. (13)
Mother is happy with her child's lisps;

Hari likewise is pleased with devotees' praise.
Shuns disrespect to his devotees. Didn't He
Slight Duryodhana by dining not with him but Vidura (14)
Remembers not the faults of His worshippers;
He is auspicious, eternal joy incarnate, world
Renowned; He accepts what is offered. Though
A mine of blessings Himself blesses people
With limitless happiness. (15)
How merciful is Hari, how devoted to His servants;
Who can narrate His activities?
Creates the world at will, protects devotees
Placing them in heaven and granting solace. (16)
King when happy gifts wealth, vehicle, jewellery
Clothes and land. Who on earth lives who
Gifts body and mind? Hari, the noble Lord,
Grants His devotees a place in heaven and
Vaikuntha; yet He is enslaved to them like a child. (17)

(Jagannath Dasa describes the Lord's unlimited greatness, sanctity and merit. He assumes different forms to save the good and punish the wicked.)

Hari's story makes holy the entire world;
It's meritorious saga of purity; is praised by Bramha and others.
Sky-blue tinged Lord is multiformed;
In the past fooled Shiva with His female-form,1 yet saved him.
Who on earth would escape Hari's magic (18)

(Notes 1 : As requested by gods Hari assumed the form of Mohini, the most beautiful woman. Mohini was moving to approach the place of nectar distribution and was dancing and producing lilting music to attract everyone. Rudra (Shiva) did not know that Shri Hari had assumed the female form. Smitten by love even in Parvati's presence Rudra extended his arms to embrace Mohini. A sudden breeze stripped off her clothes. Mohini's naked body generated greater lust and Shiva ran after her who though very close used to shy away. In his over-heated lust Shiva dropped his semen. Then he realised who Mohini was and repenting his action sought Hari's pardon. The generous Lord did pardon him.)

None in the world to forgive
Sins like Laxmi's consort; did Hari

Ever punish Indra, Moon, Tara, Bhrugu
Shiva and others for their demerits? He
Indeed is an ocean of mercy. (12)

Ganga born from toe purifies sins of mortals;
No surprise if Bhagawan's name sanctifies
Hari's name pervades Lord's body parts,
spread from head to toe; the name is revered
By Rama, Laxmi-incarnate and touching
All parts of the world. Will it not purify us? (20)
In heaven Kamadhenu (wish fulfilling cow),
wish-offering tree, Chintamani grant desired gifts;
But Mukund's most auspicious name
Lifts even those in hell;
Ignorant become wise and prosperous in the world. (21)

Should one offer Him even imaginary good things
He accepts them and in turn returns heaps,
Like Ganga water mass, giving delicious fruits.
Wearing the sins of those who have arrogated
His greatness, purifies and protects them. (22)
Hari, different from mortals, newest of the new
Most beautiful among the beautiful, sweetest
Of the sweet, the one and only handsome,
Having a golden belly is incomparable. He,
Our father, spread among Rudra and others
Lives on earth and makes us play. (23)

Parents remove their child's fears and
Make it happy at home; Indira's consort
Likewise moving around His devotee
Protects him on all sides. (24)

Devotee-dependent Hari leaves us not even for a second
Moving with us like our own shadows;
Removing difficulties offers our desired
Wishes and behaves always like us. (25)

(After extolling the supreme qualities of Shri Hari, Jagannath Dasa explains how He continues His association with the good and cruelly binds those who medidate not on him. The sole desire of all mortals is to be free from the trammels of life and death cycle. To break the vicious circle of worldly existence, one has to seek the mercy of Hari. Jagannath Dasa has described both mercies and hard-heartedness of Shri Hari.)

Those that meditate on Him not He ties to worldly miseries;
Releases those who bind Hari by devotion; bind
Grants all wishes for this and the other world. (26)
Eyelashes protect eyes; hand stretches to run itches;
Teeth dig deep into fruit and offer juice to tongue;
Like that Rama hurries to His devotees' call
And readies to bless them with rewards galore. (27)

A fire to sins Hari accepts what is offered
But never abandons devotee protection. Did He get
Angry when a mountain burdened Him?[1] Didn't
He destroy enemies and grant nectar to anxious gods? (28)

(Note 1 : Vishnu assumed the form of a tortoise to carry Mandara Mountain. It was used as a churning rod to obtain nectar from the ocean. Vishnu did not lose His temper because the mountain was placed on Him.)

Shri Hari is prepared to do anything for His devotees. He became a charioteer to Arjuna, a man-lion for Pralhad, a small boy for Bali and a ferocious killer in Parashuram. Hari's plans are inscrutable but that He protects His devotees is beyond doubt.)

The pure-minded Lord suffers no defeat or victory;
Protects those, trusting His prowess, worship;
Merciful Lord grants blessings galore not in the least
Remembering people's faults.

He is Matsya, Kurma, Varaha, fearful Narasimha,
Vamana, Parashuram, Rama and Krishna.
Became Budha to spoil the chastity of
Dhenuka's wives to kill him and finally
Was Kali born to protect the good and destroy the evil. (30)

Shri Hari is free of defect, fulfils all wishes,
Blue in hue, eternal and observer of Varna-Shrama,

God's friend; He is praised by Sama Veda,
Is a mass of good qualities and is
Laxmi's Consort. I salute Jagannath Vitthal
And He protects all. (31)

Canto III

LORD'S OMNIPRESENCE

(Shri Hari is all pervasive. There is no place where one cannot find Him. Jagannath Dasa begins his exposition of God's presence in the second stanza itself and in the third he extends it further. The canto is appropriately called "All Pervasive Lord".)

Hari is three-in-one Purusha, ancient,
Supreme; non-eternal Rama, Bramha and others
Worship Him; Hari is joy-in-full, knowledge-incarnate;
Understood by RigVedic Purusha Sookta,[1]
Resides in everyone spread the world over,
Yet, is non-attached, non-concerned. (1)

(Note [1] : Purush Sookta in RigVeda narrates Lord's creation of the world. He is thousand headed - Sahasra Sheersha Purusha - and has generated the entire world from His body. Lord Hari is the only indestructible Supreme Being. He has no rules, no fixed duties, no cycle of life and death. All other lesser Gods are strictly governed by Shri Hari and His pleasure.)

Female, neuter, male, earth, water, fire,
Wind, Sky, mind, Sun, Moon, all good and bad qualities
Are not Hari being away from them.
Bramha, Rudra, Indra and others have
Failed in comprehending Him. What
Then of mortals? How, pray, may I extol Him? (2)

(Shri Hari is extremely enigmatic and not easily understood. Though extending everywhere He is neither seen nor understood. The only solution to Lord's knowledge is to surrender oneself to Him and meditate on Him.)

Not fragrance, sweetness, form, touch
Sound He; yet named after them and
Gives pleasure to humans; eternal Hari
Stays in five knowledge-senses, five duty-senses,
Undergoes worldly actions for the good of His creation. (3)

(Paradoxically Shri Hari is everywhere and nowhere. Pralhad saw Him in pillars, beams and in every place. But his father, Hiranyakashyap, could not realise it. So he kicked a pillar and Hari revealed Himself in the form of a Man-lion to end his life of wickedness. God is therefore everywhere and yet nowhere. Jagannath Dasa elaborates on the Bhagawat idea of the Supreme Being appearing and blessing only the devoted. He is unattached to anything, non-duty-bound, non-performing. Jagannath Dasa tries to describe the concept of Hari's illusiveness in the canto.)

In ears, eyes, nose, skin, tongue, mouth,
Legs and their qualities and in gods of the bodyparts,
Shri Hari performs many duties, makes others do them;
Journeys mortals from earth, heaven and hell. (4)

Though in three qualities and in three qualifieds,[1]
Yet Hari is non-bound. Pervading from mortals
To Bramha and others Hari removes their sins.
Swallows everything in deluge, Himself remaining
undestroyed. (5)

(Note [1] : People who bear the three qualities of goodness, neither good-nor-bad and wickedness, are the qualified mortals.)

Called Aniruddha He is in every mind,
Is Pradyumna, Sankarshana is achievement,
Vasudeva is popular; Only the learned
Realise this four-fold Lord. (6)

(Hari is mind, body, achievement and realization. He has assumed different forms, and different names. Aniruddha, Pradyumna, Sankarshana and Vasudeva are different names given to Hari to identify His varied activities. Jagannath Dasa sights Hari in a multifaceted way, residing everywhere, assuming different forms and bearing different names.)

Hari shines in lotus-hearted throne;
Narayan reveals in four forms, Aniruddha and others;
Himself servant and master; receives
Service through gods with His own form in them. (7)

Hari separates in many forms man's
Sleep and Woken condition and grants
Them their deserving blessings; in sleep
Hari amasses all lives at one place like a river joining sea.
(8)

In the mortal world Shri Hari with His wives
Makes and is made by many forms
Like thread in cloth; grants rewards and
Punishments by His authority like Sun's rays.
Fools realise not Lord's magic and enchantment. (9)

(Mortal world is a place for Shri Hari's activities. He assumes human forms, behaves like human beings and has a family like human beings. But all this seemingly human appearance is a show for man to watch. Shri Hari is, indeed, free from everything. Jagannath Dasa vividly explains Hari's position among gods, men and the rest of the world. In fact, it is Hari's story. Harikatha is nothing but His epic saga narrating His supremacy, prowess and greatness.)

Father dresses his son in costly silk and jewellery
Gets him salute and blesses him. He is happy.
Likewise Shri Hari is the one both revered and
Worshipper; makes worship material Himself.
And grants his devotees all the fruits of worship. (10)

(Shri Hari is a master actor in a one-man show. He produces articles for worship, makes someone worship and stands Himself as an object of worship. With His activities being the worshipper the worshipped and the worshipping material He does not get the reward for Himself. All the fruits of good deeds are transferred to His devotees. That shows God, the merciful)

Father celebrates his son's wedding in style
With friends and relatives and places him
In the house. Like that Indira's Consort creates
Three-qualitied mortals and binds them
To joy and sorrow mixed world. (11)

Smoke surrounds inside a grass hut
Peeps out through holes to reveal fire;
Shri Hari, similarly, is inside and out
In the worldly creatures and makes good
And bad actions with no one seeing Him. (12)

(In all these stanzas Jagannath Dasa mentions Shri Hari's activities in the world, His creation. Hari is invisibly present everywhere and is responsible for all actions. Jagannath Dasa excels in his literary style by emphasizing Shri Hari's supremacy in a number of home-spun simple examples. Father and son, fire and hut, tree and branches are so familiar to every reader that he enjoys Hari's story the way he does the best home-made food. The writer has a vast experience of the world and with his observant eye catches to picture the kaleidoscopic beauties of his familiar world.)

When watered at the roots tree sprouts into branches and fruits;
Likewise Lord accepts people's offerings
Grants blessings in the name of Bramha, Rudra and others;
Never does He reveal that He has given them. (13)

Shri Hari is unreachable by Vedas, incalculably great,
Has no birth, is joy incarnate, indestructible,
Omnipresent, supporter of the world; Rama's
Consort is Bramha's father. He moves in others
Enjoys the positions of master and servant. (14)

Hari fixes people's mind on worldly matters
Establishes world's joys in it making them
Appear new and fully satisfying. People
Remember not the Lord even in dream.
Thus pervades Hari in all His creations. (15)

He, the promoter, hides in mind and body
To enjoy worldly pleasures. Hari, fortune incarnate,
Himself offers and receives; with
No one's knowledge enjoys through each body
And expresses His pleasure. (16)

Hari is eternal, beyond the ken of Vedas
Free of qualities, devotee-dear, destroyer of fear,
Wedded to truth, fit for reverence and blue hued beauty.
Such a Lord moves like an intoxicated person
Entering bodies and leaving them. He thus is
Everywhere close to His devotees. (17)

Madhav brilliant extraordinarily like blue diamond,
Coral resides in gods, demons and mortals;
Makes them work according to their qualities.
He hidden in Vayu and other gods shows
Himself to enjoy fruits of actions. (18)

Smallest of the small, biggest of the big
The biggest in the smallest, is Hari.
The lightest is sunk, the heaviest floated;
This is Hari's wizardry. What could demons'
Anger do? Like a pestle in the pounding pit
Separates chaff from grain, Hari destroys bodies
And creates mortals' souls. (19)

Gods, demons and men always exist.
Hari shows them no love, indifference or hatred.
Depending on their merit though Hari grants
Happiness to gods, misery to demons and
Sorrow to men. He enjoys nothing; He is beyond everything.
(20)

Hari is present where people sing about Him,
Present in idols, present in blessings, of gods,
Everywhere one runs or one plays is Hari ever present.
Wisest of the wise, hates the wicked; being
Lord of the world who can equal Shri Hari? (21)

Redhot iron looks like fire; when cool
Is iron again. Since Hari is present among all,
Everyone, always He is related, lives normally. (22)

When it rains trees grow, bear fruits of different
Taste and juice. Likewise lives Laxmi's consort
In different lives granting blessings to suit
Their actions. Where, pray, is His discrimination? (23)

Sun's rays make diamonds shine different hues,
Changing no colour yet bright to the sight;
Thus again moves Hari in lives making
No change but granting reward related to actions. (24)

Like tolling the hour by pushing a bell in place of
Water time measure Hari, Himself a doer, distributes
Results of actions or merit and demerit. He makes them
Enjoy them standing Himself as a witness. (25)

Hari unattached lives with worldly beings;
Makes them to their work, does like them Himself;
But leaves the fruit to them, not to Himself;
Hari like the sky is spread all over
Not minding small, big, pot or drum. (26)

When hit hot not fire but iron has the pain;
Likewise Lord in heated way resides in beings inside and outside,
How could their sufferings affect Him? (27)

Children builds and houses, play with them awhile,
Destroy them joyfully after; the same way
Hari creates worlds, protects them. (destroys, too)
Snake swallows its own eggs; likewise what
Pleasure or pain can touch Hari? (28)

(Shakespeare said "World's a stage, we are all actors." It is true that we are actors. But Jagannath Dasa says that Shri Hari is Himself an actor and director. He wears different dress to suit His role. He still is an unconcerned actor, noncommittal, nonparticipant, non-existing. Jagannath Dasa establishes the ever present Hari's varied actions and points out how human beings are a toy in His hands. It is He who breaks them, works them and gets them worked. He is the doer, the deed and the agent. His devotees understand His greatness and are His servants.)

Shri Hari is pure, full of joy, intelligent,
Defectless; He like an actor wears costume
Fools people by His eloquence; puts on
Many forms, lands on the earth; granting
Blessings makes humans happy. (29)

A wicked man by magic craft can
Make water and fire do no harm to him.
How could sins and merits, time, qualities three
Bind Him who has the world in His belly;
Resides in every heart and is free from defect? (30)

In Hari are hidden many qualities in one;
In one world are many; He is inside and out
In all beings like the sky all spread; He is

Known by many names, is fully joyful;
It is He who makes others do their actions. (31)

Jagannath Vitthal, super warrior, Love God's father,
Killer of demons resides among all
Makes all reside in Him. He knows world's
Beginning, middle and end.
With His devotee's suffering out
He came from pillar. (32)

Canto IV

FOOD CONTENT DIVISION

(Human beings, especially, and all living animals in the world consume food to live. Food is God and food is sacred. Before it is consumed people offer it to the Creator because it is He who has made it and made it possible for people to eat it. God is "Anna Maya" (lives in food) and is to be honoured. He resides in food.

People eat four types of food - Khadya (food that is chewed) Choushya (swallowed food) Peya (liquid that is drunk) Lehya (food that is licked by tongue). Hari lives in the four types, assumes juicy form and eats it Himself and makes others eat, too. Human beings should realise divine presence in food and consume it.

Jagannath Dasa narrates Hari's extensive appearance in human activities, even his food.)

Four types of food world people eat
Hari lives in them in four juicy forms
Builds their body eating to their taste;
Limbs developed joyfully, the knowledge-eager
Shown His presence. (1)

Shri Hari resides in seventytwo vein-gods
Supports sixteen limbs of our nest-like body;
Hari surreptitiously fosters and Himself moves joyfully in the world. (2)

Water God lives as six watery-juices, thirty six
Veins in men and women and called
Brahati. He roams around the world day and night. (3)

Six juices with three qualities are eighteen;
With contact of Sara, Asara, Neeta Aprachura,
Khanda Akhanda and Chit Prachura[1] become seventytwo thousand;
Laxmi's consort bearing these names resides in

Our body and food; meditate on Him and eat. (4)

(Note [1] : There are three qualities or Gunas. One is good (Satwika), "indifferent" (Rajasa) and bad (Tamasa) and each human being has a combination of these qualities. Some have more of good quality and become good people, afraid of committing sins and bent on leading a good life. Others have more of indifferent quality and are middlings in respect of goodness and wickedness. Still others have more of bad or wicked quality. They always indulge in sin and destruction. Sages and gods are Satwika-oriented, ordinary humans Rajasa-oriented and demons Tamasa-oriented. By Hari's grace His devotees try to increase their good qualities.

It is believed, and perhaps correctly that man's food is responsible for the qualities. They are therefore advised to avoid Tamasa food.

Sara is half quality and half indifferent quality.

Asara is more of bad quality. It may have some element of indifferent quality. Sara and Asara together are one part of eighteen things.

Neeta is sweet or tongue-satisfying food. Aprachura is sweet, salt and hot and unrecognised bitterness.

Khanda is mixing sour with salt and hot. A little sweet is Akhanda. Both these form another unit.

Sara is good for god's devotees and brings pleasure to them. So, it is called Chit.

Tamasa, Rajasa, food is appreciated by low people and is called Prachura.

These form a part of 18 juices half of it good, half indifferent and bad).

(A reader easily notices how frequently Jagannath Dasa uses arithmetic numbers. "Aarumooredondu Saavira", "Shodashatmaka", "Eppatteradu Saavira" etc are some examples to illustrate the point. In fact, Indian philosophy revels in number game and Lord Vishnu has one thousand names, Shri Raghavendra Swami prayer is "Ashtottara" and many other religious activities are number oriented. Of special note is is Jagannath Dasa's numerous references to numbers.)

In milk juices 354, in good ghee 29, in tasty jaggery 5001;
In fruits 2825; meditate that God is in these forms. (5)
Contemplating on the Lord in all juices 8309 resides Shri Hari;
Four main jucies in milk, ghee, jaggery and fruit
Contain 8309 forms of the Lord; Chittabhimani and Tatwabhmani[1] gods;

Lord is present in wise people's home and they meditate on
Him. (6)

(Note [1] : Chittabhimani is Vayu and he resides in 24 Tatwesha or Tatwabhimani demi-gods. When a devotee while eating meditates on gods residing in food, he will feel the presence of the Almighty around him.)

Kapila in eyes, Narasimha on nose-tip, in
Mouth Parashurama, on Tongue Matsya and
Swan reside in teeth. Hari, the eternal, and bearing many names, lives
In these forms in man's limbs and having
Enjoyed pleasures offers them fruit. (7)
Shri Hari of infinite happiness resides in
Diners in the form of Sankarshana, Pradyumna to give strength.
He feeds man to satisfaction as Narayana and Aniruddha. (8)

With Rama Vasudeva joyfully stays in five forms inside
And outside and in sky
To help His creations to breathe.
Bramha, Rudra, Indra, other gods, demons
And man are an abode of Hari.
Thus contemplate wise people. (9)

In rice is Vasudeva, in five delicious eats is Sankarshana,
Pradyumna in pudding, and Aniruddha in ghee
(Payasa)
Krishna is in soup, Upendra in vegetables
The main Narayana resides in all food. (10)

Myriad formed Hari resides fully in good food,
In every bit individually, makes humans happy.
Offer food to Him knowing different forms and His main indivisible form. (11)

Such a diner is a daily worshipper, healthy,
Sinless, earns merit of many sacrifice-offerings.
Uncertain things are firm, arrive in
Rama's consort. This merciful Lord listens to you like your mother does. (12)

Twice six thousand two hundred and twentyone formed
Aniruddha is in food. Thrice two thousand fortythree
Formed Pradyumna lives as life-giver on earth. (13)

Sinless Sankarshana exists inside outside life sheath
In 562107 forms. He is called Manomaya. (14)

Called Vijnanamaya Vasudeva lives in
Four thousand three seventyfour forms spreading in
All connected gods. River Viraja, Rama incarnate, born of auspicious
Lord (Purusha) breaks[1] bodies of god-oriented people. (15)

(Note [1] : The river Viraja is believed to give permanent release from the world. Devotees who are concentrated on god are released from their bodies to reach heaven.)

Narayana assumes five thousand hundred twenty five forms
Is a mass of joy every day.
He has spread on earth in five lakh eightyfive
Thousand four hundred forms. (16)

Shanti's consort is food-spread in hundred one forms;
Pradyumna is life-giving in five thirteen forms;
Sankarshana resides in fiftyfive forms in fickle minds;
Vasudeva, spreading over the whole world
Is Vijnana form in hundred eightyfour ways. (17)

God named Narayana entering body in three
Thousand fiftytwo forms is joyful.
Like ghee hiding in butter Shri Hari is hiding
In four thousand three hundred five forms in Pranesh (Vayu). (18)

In a body of life-breath (Prana Vayu) Aniruddha
Resides in fiftythree forms; in Apana life
Pradyumna lives in five hundred one forms;
Vyana named life contains Sankarshana in
Fiftyfive forms; in Udana life resides Vasudeva
In five hundred thirtyfive forms. (19)

Basic form of Narayana resides assuming
Five hundred fiftyseven forms among all
Humans in equal proportion. Hari
Bearing a thousand seven hundred eleven shapes
Plays in the world. (20)

Hari performs Shraddhas as Aniruddha in ninety three forms;
Always as master Pradyumna fire, Yama, Moon and other gods
Are fed; as Sankarshana feeds Himself and others
A share offered to ancestors; as Vasudeva grants
Food and physical pleasure. (21)

The ninety-six formed Hari resides in Vasus,
Rudras, Suns and others. Accepts the devotees'
Pure supplication; the merciful Lord grants unlimited
Happiness to ancestors and protects them. (22)

As sun Hari is in fiftyone alphabets; twelve petals
Of heart-lotus, twentyfour tenets, seven metals.
Aniruddha always supports life. Wise therefore
Should realise and worship the ninetysix formed Lord. (23)

Lord bearing the world in His belly ate
Shabari's [1] once-tasted fruits; gave pleasure to
Gopikas; ate what sages' wives offered. Though
Over-ornamented accepted Kubja's [2] unguents
To grant bodily pleasure. Hari, served by gods and
Sages, will surely accept devotees' sincere offerings. (24)

(Note [1] : This refers to Ramayan story where a simple god-fearing woman devoted to Rama had collected berries to offer to Rama. To sort out the rotten fruits from the best Shabari tasted them herself first and kept the best for Rama, Sita and Laxmana.

Note [2] : A deformed Kubja used to carry perfumes or unguents to Kamsa. One day Krishna and Balarama met her and asked for some perfume. She readily offered it to the Lord. The deformed Kubja was transformed as beautiful lady and had Krishna's blessings.)

Lord's joy and merits are innumerable; Rama,
Bramha, Indras' deeds are nothing.
When man eats every morsel of food as if offered

To Krishna, He extends
His hand like a child to a feeding mother. (25)

Human actions are accepted and Rama's consort
Blesses them related to good deeds. Fire
Burns everything with no feeling.
Likewise Shri Hari superpurifies the pure.
Is there any wonder in a natural happening? (26)

Sick tongue finds good food and water bitter.
Healthy tongue finds them tasty. An eternally
Healthy Being finds everything, everytime good and delicious.
Will not Krishna who sucked Putana's poisonous
Breast-milk accept our devotedly offered gifts? (27)

How can I describe? Vayu protected the world
After drinking deadly Kalakuta poison. He therefore
Is called "Amruta". Laxmi's Consort accepts human's
Sins and merits, yet He has no birth nor death.
Eternal joy alone is His food. (28)

Remember that it's He, promoter, omnipresent
That resides in different forms in life-giving food.
Lay at His door your deeds, good and bad
And leave the result to Him. (29)

Jagannath Vitthal, Lord of Shridevi, Bhoodevi and Durga,
Assumes fiftyeight lakh nine thousand sevenhundred
Five forms in all food and Himself accepts it.
Spreading from head to toe in mortal bodies
He offers protection. (30)

Canto V

LORD'S DIVINITY EVERYWHERE

(This canto is called "Vibhuti" canto. Vibhuti refers to prosperity and divine presence. Lord's divine presence is felt in His manifestations involving knowledge, desire and work. Hari's power is felt in all animate and inanimate creations. Depending on the appearance, purpose and abilities Lord is found in all creations. He makes them perform nonhuman activities, show super strength and extraordinariness. Shri Hari therefore has to be understood, worshipped and honoured. His grace should be humbly sought.)

Watch happily Laxmi's consort's divine forms
Neeta, Sadharana, Visheshana, Sajati, Naija
Ahita, Sahaja, Vijati, Khanda, Akhanda are ten, [1]
Say the wise. Learn them, meditate on them
Always, everywhere and watch with pleasure. (1)

(Note [1] : Shri Hari exhibits His divine manifestation in different earthly forms. His devotees should realise this and surrender themselves to Him.

Neeta Vibhuti is in Shaligram stones.
Sadharana Vibhuti is in Brahmins and house-holders
Visheshana or Vishesha Vibhuti is in ascetics.
Sajati Vibhuti is in Shankara, Indra.
Naija Vibhuti is in Lord's incarnation such as
Rama, Krishna.
Ahita Vibhuti is in tall mountains and peaks.
Sahaja Vibhuti lies in the best among the same kind.
Vijati Vibhuti is in the moon among stars as
Lion is among animals.
Understanding divinity in things is Khanda
Vibhuti.
Understanding divinity spread in one form alone
is Akhanda Vibhuti.

Jagannath Dasa in this canto echoes the sermon that Krishna gave to Arjuna in the Bhagawat Geeta. Divinity is not in one particular place, form or person. Hari is omnipresent, awe-inspiring and fantastic. Devotees have to understand His greatness.)

Hari has created many lives in water, ground and sky.
Sajati, Vijati, Sadharana, Visheshana contain
His presence. Meditate on Him and joyfully worship. (2)

Hari's divine presence is in Shaligram,
Moving forms, cows, guests, basil Ashwattha,
Unknown people that come at dinner time,
Ascetics, forest-dwellers, householders, bachelors,
Officials, relatives, and others, He resides in
Ground, water, fire, wind, sky, planets,
Yoga, Karna, stars, day, fortnights. (3)

Like shining burning gold, Laxmi's consort
Stays everyday in Shaligram in five thousand five hundred thirtyfive forms;
And always in mountain-lovers like
Garuda, Shesha and Rudra. (4)

Hari in five hundred thirteen forms is
In moving idols, and in temple idols suited
To His divinity. To devotees He is present
As fire in forest wood. (5)

Maker of sense-organs Hari assumes 52114
Forms in articles of worship. He runs to
Accept worship of those who know His forms
Like a thirsty man dying to drink water. (6)

Know Hari's forms in non-moving things, in
Bramha and others. Forget rewards, enjoy
Food and shelter given by Him and worship the Lord. (7)

God has 24 forms in water, 5317 in basil,
162 in flowers, 13 in lamps, 402 in beautiful
Idols and sandal. (8)

Hari, defectless, entire joy, supreme in prowess,
Resides in lotus-petalled heart of mortals.

Punishes the wicked; increases religious devotion
Among honest and wise followers. (devotees). (9)

In wealth, body, house, family and friends; in
Good qualities, mind, ego, sense organs and
Work organs is Hari present under different names.
Remember He works and makes one work. (10)

Think of duality in Bhava, Dravya and Kriya; [1]
Forget Him not always and everywhere;
Feelings self to be His worship Hari. He sure will
Be physically seen. Merciful Lord protects you
Like He did Gajendra. (11)

(Note [1] : Bhavadvaita or duality in Bhava is the difference one finds in each thread and the mass of threads that go to make cloth. Like thread and cloth Shri Hari spreads in the world individually in things and collectively in His creation. Such a duality is Bhava duality. Duality in Dravya lies in one's doing good deeds, helping others but fully knowing Hari's presence everywhere and offering one's good deeds to Him. Kriya duality is renouncing individual existence. One lives, works and prays because of divine presence and grace. If a person thinks thus he realises the duality in Kriya.)

Articles of worship, new and varied, reside
In sky and other elements. Remember them
Meditate on them; worship Govind and
Enjoy His presence. (12)

Fix Hari's form firmly in mind, worship
Him whether cold, heat, rain or wind. Believe that
Earth's smell is fragrance water is juice,
Fire a lamp, wind a fan and words are music.
Offer them to Hari and He will be pleased. (13)

Think your body a temple of Hari, wash it clean.
Body parts are lamps, their action a mattress,
Pleasure a cover, confession a cloth. (14)

Our sins are shoes, merit and invocation a perfume,
Clear mind a basil, actions flowers,
Anger incense, devotion many ornaments,

Knowledge an umbrella, wisdom a light,
Finally Hari story is a waving of lights. (15)

Offer to Hari everyday as temple perambulation,
Your actions done by body, speech and mind.
Remember this as the best; the wise know it. (16)

To obtain merit (Purusharth) nothing in
World equals this, no Shastra says "No".
Hari who exists in sense-pleasures is pleased
When one offers all he has in the form of worship. (17)

Body is fireplace; senses are fire, things cropping up are woodsticks,
Effort is wind; lust smoke, the together two is flame.
Excess pleasure are sparks, words uttered
Are "mantras" and thinking is sacrifice. (18)

(In all these stanzas Jagannath Dasa emphasizes how one can surrender everything to God. He should consider himself to be in Hari's service, body, speech and mind. Body is itself a temple with five senses at the Lord's service. A mortal who realizes Hari's presence everywhere and considers himself totally dedicated or offered has a chance of seeing Lord's physical presence and obtaining His blessings.)

To madhu-killer our body is a town;
Eyes, nostrils and mouth are eastern doors;
Ears are north-south gates; arms and sex-organs
Western doors; heart-lotus is Lord's house.
Chest is arch and three qualities arch pots (Kalasha) (19)

Body ingredients are seven forts, veins small lanes,
Flesh elephants, spine is the main street; Hair is forest;
In this Vayu, a watchman, assumes five forms to kill enemies. (20)

Sun, moon and other gods work as Hari's doorkeepers,
Desires are soldiers, pleasures themselves
For the body-town are decorated shops. Life is
A merchant and the Lord receives royalty from him. (21)

In Hari's mansion ten senses [1] are a line of mirrors,

Breath a fan, intellect a charming woman
Sleep is prostrating before the Lord. (22)

(Note [1] : The ten senses are - five mental faculties and five physical faculties. The five mental faculties are senses of perception. They are skin, tongue, eyes, ear and nose. Karmendriya are organs of action. They are also five, speech (mouth), hands, feet, laps and the trunk. In all there are ten organs.)

Mouth, a palacedoor, has moustache as festoons.
Hair flying paper, feet, bones, thighs, waist,
Belly, head are terraces and five sheaths are
Rooms. So should one worship Him. (23)

Our body is a chariot, our clothes flags;
Ten marks on body are flag posts. Mental
Control is a throne; good thoughts are Kalasha;
Three qualities are horse-reins and whip; deeds done are
wheels;
Ten organs are swift steed. Thus should one worship. (24)

Believe Vayu to be a chariot, Shri Hari the rider;
Protecting body from cold, wind and heat give up
All your love for it; then you will be a great Yogi. (25)

In the ocean of life, in the river of sin and merit,
Make body arriving with birth and death a boat;
Think Laxmi's consort with His people is enjoying;
Meditated thus on god, Vayu's father Shri Hari
Will release us from ocean of existence and give
happiness. (26)

Food in shops and home, people's ornaments,
Oil for burning are for Lord's sacrifice.
Forget this not and live like a king unafraid. (27)

World a huge pedestal, Meru is throne,
Bhagirathi is holy water, directions clothes
Speech incantation, self-grown fruits and vegetables
An offering, wind a fragrance, sun and moon
Are lamps, stars are ornaments - all for
Hari's service. He accepts them and blesses. (28)

(Shri Hari lives in all people of all castes. The four caste people are equally acceptable to Him. Brahmins, Kshatriyas, Vaishya and Shudra are the repositories of the Lord. He is in them some of Himself and directs them to do their work.)

Bramha in Brahmins has Vasudeva. Vayu, Garuda,
Rudra, Shesha, Indra, Sun, Moon, Love, God, Fire,
Water-God and others reside in Kshatriyas.
They watch Sankarshana and are happy. (29)

Aniruddha, Love-God's son, Prana, Apana, Vyana,
Udana, and other 49 Marudganas, Rudragana,
Vasugana, Ganapati, Vishwaksena, Kubera and others
Reside in Vaishyas and should worship Pradyumna. (30)

Ashwini, Nijaruti protector of directions, Yama,
Yama's servants, earth, death, Shani are present in Shudras.
Think that Aniruddha lives in them. (31)

Narayana of four-caste Lord, makes each one his
Stipulated duty and is responsible for it. He is
like warp and weft among all and grants them
happiness. (32)

(Jagannath Das has always extolled the supreme qualities of God. God is extraordinary, a mountain of joy, fearless and a terrible destroyer. Yet He is equal to all and is praised for His fairness and impartiality. Jagannath Dasa very often emphasizes these super human qualities of God.)

Destroyer, grantor of wealth, creator extraordinary,
Hari is yet equal among all and is extolled so.
Lover of Sama Veda, worshipped by Gods, Vaikuntha dweller,
Bearing names of Parashurama, Hayavadana, Shri Hari is
present in all.
Meditate on Him thus to know him. (33)

In a mirror one looks turned left to right, right to left;
Likewise to Aniruddha the world looks different.
Man, a reflection of Him, should know it and worship.
Only then does Lord accept his offerings. (34)

Better people are the real; lower in knowledge are reflections;

The real is Hari; sing, worship wear ornaments,
Give in charity and enjoy, thinking everything
To be the service of the Lotus-eyed Lord. (35)

Like river water used for Puja thrown back in river
Lord's things be given back to Him. Abandoning the feeling
"I have done it," "I've made and left", surrender self to Him.
Like a spoon [1] useful for all Shri Hari is behind all. (36)

(Note [1] : A simile relating man's actions to the existence of Hari is very appropriate. A spoon is just an instrument not a doer. It dips into everything if someone pushes it. A spoon is not independent. Man, too, is not independent. He should firmly accept the fact that he is just a tool in the hands of the Lord. He, like the spoon, does what Hari makes him to.)

Rain water flows whether we see or not see.
If people know it they will bathe with pleasure.
Likewise Hari accepts pleasures of life residing in us.
Wise people offer them and earn eternal bliss. (37)

All our doings unhesitatingly be offered to Srinivasa.
He takes them to grant happiness. Like a cow
Eating grass, drinking water gives milk,
Shri Hari grants blessings to His devotees. (38)

In east, south, west, north, in Ishanya Parvati's
Consort's abode, Agneya, Vayavya, Nairutya,[1]
In all directions resides Hamsa-named Lord.
Always, among all Hari exists unseen and as
He wishes. (39)

(Note [1] : Agneya, Vayavya, Ishanya, Nairutya are all the four other directions - other than east, west, north and south. Each direction is presided over by a deity. Ishanya has Shiva, Agneya has fire or Agni, Vayavya has Vayu or Wind-God and Nairutya has a demon named Niruti.)

Thus Idavatsara in five years bears Aniruddha form.
Has five names Barhaspatya, Sauramana,
Nakshatramana, Chandramana and another Sauramana.
Omnipotent Jagannath Vitthal protects
Those who remember Him by granting
blessings suitably. (40)

Canto VI

FIVE BIG SACRIFICES

(The sixth canto is called "Pancha Maha Yojna" and also "Panchagni Hotra". In the world movements and activities centre on five fires or energies. Fire is an essential part of any sacrifice. It is energy and exists in the world in various forms especially in five main forms. The five fires or energies are Dyu, Parjanya, Dhara, Purush and Stree (Sky, Rain, Earth, Man and Woman). Some writers attribute these energies to fires - to Mother, Father, Earth, Cloud and Sky. In all these God's presence is felt by a devotee. Aniruddha and other gods are the presiding deities. Mother has Aniruddha fire, this Aniruddha being Aniruddha Aniruddha, Aniruddha Pradyumna, Aniruddha Sankarshana, Aniruddha Vasudeva, Aniruddha Narayana. All these are in one form only. Similarly Pradyumna is in Father again having Pradyumna Aniruddha etc. All these generate life and protect the world. Jagannath Dasa has vividly narrated the making of the world and the relationship god has with man and His creation.)

Think of Narayana's thirty forms as five
Fires in Mother, father, earth, sky and cloud.
Meditate on His activities making each day
As a sacrificial fire and ask for
Total release from the world. (1)

Sky is a fire, sun firewood, his rays smoke,
Day flames, stars sparks, moon fire;
In such Moon are five forms of Narayana.
Make a sacrifice with incantation in devotional talk. (2)

Fire is cloudproud, wood is Wind-god, smoke is a line of clouds;
Lightening is flame, thunder is spark and ash.
Wise men devotionally sacrifice for lives reached the moon in such fire. (3)
Earth is fire, years wood, sky smoke, night flams;

Directions are burning pieces, rain is sacrificial offering;
Think thus; pleasing Hari meditate on red form and enjoy
leadership. (4)

(Jagannath Dasa delves deep into highly technical matter of cosmology. His analysis of the world is rcal and intellectually satisfying. In many stanzas he points out by examples the metaphors in a sacrifice and how man a creation of God has to humbly surrender to God.)

Purusha is fire, our speech is wood, hearing smoke,
Tongue flames, ears sparks, eyes ashes; believing thus
Offer our food to Krishna as sacrificial offering.
He will accept it and protect us. (5)

In woman waist is wood, lustful talk smoke,
Vagina big flame, fire pieces are the act of entering it;
Love games are sparks, ejaculation is sacrificial offering
To Hari; if done so, the Lord accepting it pardons sins. (6)

(Even a sexual act has its dignity and philosophical significance. Woman is one of the five fires. Aniruddha, Narayana, Vasudeva and Sankarshana are the repositories of different love-acts. If man offers everything to Hari, He will remove his sins.

Jagannath Dasa very vividly explains the metaphorical significance of love-act and considers it as a sacrifice offered to Hari. Lord Krishna is all-pervading. Every action of man should be focussed on Him.)

No rebirth to one who remembers five-formed Hari's
Twentyfive forms in five fires. As He protected
Arjuna in Kurukshetra, released Shishupala
Who had insulted Him, the fear-remover Lord
will support. (7)

Like five-women horse [1] Hari of five forms
Has thirty different forms. With different names
Hari is in five fires. The three qualities assigned
To five type beings [2] have Lord's play. (8)

(Note [1] : This is collecting five women, arranging them with their legs and hands to show horses' tail and legs. This is what Jagannath Dass calls "Panchanarituraga". Like the five horse show is Hari with five different forms.

Note [2] : The five type being are Deva, Gandharva, Pitru, Manushya, Asura. They are gods, semi-gods, ancestors, men and demons.)

Hari is in everyone's heart including Bramha and Rudra

The Original formed Padmanabha, Achyuta and others
Reside in myriad in Adibhoots, Adhyatma and Adidaivata.
Prana, Apana and other five forms, Naga and
Other five sub-forms are Hari's ten different forms. (9)

Wisc people should meditate daily on 10326
Forms in four places. Hari lives in ten beings
In 18127 forms and is called by different names. (10)

In all are 28453 forms. Realising the significance
Of ten forms in four places a devotee should worship. (11)

(Jagannath Dasa has narrated the extent of Shri Hari's presence in the world. He has vividly enumerated how He, in various forms, resides in the world and His creations. A good devotee will understand the all-pervasive nature of the Lord and worship Him with single-minded devotion. Then only he obtains release from the worldly miseries.)

Vayu, in the form of Naga (snake), resides
With 16416 forms in living beings. Durga's consort
Lord of Tamas, is with Vayu but gives sense
Organs wrong Knowledge, false love and other bad
qualities. (12)

Hari wearing five forms as Kruddolka, [1] Maholka,
Virolka, Dyulka, Sahasrolka, resides hiding
In five-Prana place that create five disciplines.
Removes evil knowledge of the good, and bestows
False knowledge to the wicked. (13)

(Note [1] : The five disciplines are traditional. They are Tarka (logic) Vyakarna (grammar) Meemamsa (investigation or enquiry) Chhandas (Prosody) and Alankara (Poetics or Figurative Writing). Shri Hari is a patron of knowledge and resides in all forms of intellectual activities. He, therefore, assumes different forms to reside in all disciplines of human knowledge. He is kind to the good people and removes their ignorance. It is, however, difficult for the evil-minded to understand God and they succeed in increasing their ignorance. Tamas is a road to ignorance leading to wickedness.)

He is in cows as Udgeetha; in sheep and goats
As Vrastava and Hinkara; in horses as Pratihara;
In man as Nidhana; One who meditates thus on
Him, the originator of Vedas, will have no rebirth. (14)

He is in four Yuga (age) and directs appropriate duties;
As Vasudeva He is Yugadikrut (maker of Yuga);
Being a source of Dharma, Hari grants
His devotees prosperity, knowledge and wealth. (15)

Narayana in head, Vasudeva below throat above chest
On right Pradyumna, on left Aniruddha, below
Waist is Sankarshana. Hari's five forms in body
Be remembered. (16)

Narayana spread in the whole body; Sankarshana
From waist to feet; from head to stomach at the back
Vasudeva;

Aniruddha in front and left; Pradyumna of right;
Meditate thus, you are free from impurity,
Any duty and any rule; (17)

Padmanabh is in hands, Hrushikesha in mouth,
Shridhara in nostrils, Vamana in tongue,
Trivikrama in soft skin, Madhusudana in eyes;
And Vishnu resides in ears. (18)

Govinda in mind, Madhava in physical love;
Narayana in great principles; Keshav in unseen principles;
God's presence in body makes good people indeed deified.
(19)

In land as Krishna; in water as Hari;
In fire Parashurama and Upendra; in wind Janardana;
In sky as Achyuta; in sandal Narasimha;
In juice shines Hari as Adhokhsaja. (20)

In beauty is Purushottama, in touch Aniruddha;
In words Pradyumna; in waste Vasudeva;
In anus Sankarshana; in feet Damodara;
These are very well established. (21)

(A reader will certainly notice a good amount of repetition in many stanzas. Either the repetition is done purposely to emphasize the point which if not done so may, perhaps, escape the devotee's notice or a couple of repetitions are interpolations of some inferior writer. The interpolations have been passed off as the great Jagannath Dasa's.

Jagannath Dasa is a master of precise thinking and clear expression. He is concise and wastes no word. This, he must have learned from Guru Raghavendra Swami whose Baconian epigrammatic style has been praised by Jagannath Dasa's preceptor, Vadeendratirtha. "Uktam no vaktibhooyah" etc -15th stanza of Guru Guna Stavana written by Vadeendratirtha, states that Raghavendra Swami would not waste words. Being trained in such discipline Jagannath Dasa would not waste his masterful words.

With all the above arguments, it is still not final to say that the repetitions are the work of a "fake" scholar.

Shripati is spread in all living bodies in 24
Forms as Aniruddha and others. Circling
Around like a creeper He is pleased with
Ancestral offerings in Shraddhas and is in
94 forms of Shraddhas. (22)

With 1152 forms Hari is spread in 24 tenet-
Presiding deities; protects all and has no
Self interest. (23)

As Shakti Indira's consort lives in eleven forms;
Grants handsome form, joy incarnate, is
Purusha and resides in humans permanently. (24)

He appears in the body in sixteen forms in sixteen parts.
All pervading Hari shines in body as the
Proficient and the fifteen forms in ten senses.
He is in sky, wind fire, water and earth, all five
elements. (25)

In mind as Atma, in ego (self) as Antaratma,
In great tenets as Paramatma, in the invisible
As Inanatma is Shri Hari. Understanding these
Fifty worded principles a devotees should worship Him. (26)

In twentyfour tenets, in Bramha and others that
Are their (tenets) patrons Aniruddha has pervaded

In 13824 forms but behaves like common people. (27)

From Keshav to Damodara twelve beautiful forms
For twelve months are present twelve Namas (caste marks)·
Vedavyasa with 5 formed Aniruddha lives in six seasons.
Meditating on this follow good conduct all the thirty days
Not expecting any reward but His mercy and praise.(28)

Tile, gold, iron, mountain, wood and other inanimate things
And Brahma and other animate beings
Are with no knowledge of them made to
Perform duties. Hari is their favourite and grants them their wishes. (29)

Vasudeva and Aniruddha are in men, Sankarashana,
Pradyumna in women; Hari praised by Shrutis
Lives in all beings. People who worship well
Are released. (30)

Merciful Lord spreading in Brahma and others
His myriad forms makes and allows them do their work.
He protects them accepting their good deeds. (31)

Only sky-spread clouds can realise sea-water
Differences, not crows and sparrows. That
The three quality-world is in Hari, Sleeper on Serpent,
Is realised by Madhva philosophers, not ignoramuses. (32)

Remember Aniruddha forms in Bramha and
Other gods, in ten senses, in three qualities
And five elements. Lord will present Himself
If praised everyday, pleased and in trance
Over Him. He will relieve you of worldly worries. (33)

Shri Narayana is in mind, in ear and
Eyes, Matsya and Kurma, Varaha in skin,
Narasimha in tongue, Vamana in nostrils,
In mouth Parashurama, in hand Rama,
Krishna in feet. Buddha who misled Jains
Is in anus and Kali, demon-destroyer in

Organs of generation. Meditating on the ten
Incarnations, offering all his work, his enjoyment
To the Lord, a devotee should praise Jagannath Vitthal.
(34 and 35)

Canto VII

BODY OF FIVE ELEMENTS

(This canto has been called "Tanuchatushtaya Sandhi" by some publishers. The canto again refers to the human body and the many parts - both external and internal - and the respective gods associated with the parts. The basic internal elements of the body that merge into nature are five - Pruthvi, Ap, Teja, Vayu and Akasha (Earth, water, light, wind and sky). The body disintegrates itself to finally join the several elements.

Each elements in the body is presided over by a deity. A true devotee clearly understands the distribution of the body and its god-presided over element. Jagannath Dasa in his usual highly intellectual comprehension has described every aspect in this canto. He uses the numbers liberally and each number is multiplied to yield an awesome figure to astound the reader of the infinite extent of god's presence in the world.)

Earth, water, fire, wind, sky, words and
Breath and others are in five-quality body
Recognised by 51 alphabets. Hari spreads
In body and blesses gods, demons. Punishes who insult. (1)

It's known that Hari, originator of Om,
Lives in three letters (a, u, m) spreading
In body as Aniruddha. He assumes 15, 21, 24
Forms respectively in Linga, Aniruddha and Sthool bodies
Lord is in 72000 veins and in Sun's rays
Shining everywhere. (2)

In Jiva, Linga, Aniruddha and Sthoolaka bodies
Lives Hari in Vishwaroopa (Universal form),
Hayagriva, Aniruddha, Narayana, Padmanabha
And in Hamsa (Swan) forms. Meditate on
Nineteen forms in the four parts of the Lord. (3)
Like all things visible clearly in a clean mirror
Hari in inanimate and living things, shines
With many forms in good men's mental mirror.

He is multiformed, independent, non-moving,
Healthy, unmoved. (4)

In four types of bodies, in five sheaths and
Seven elements spreads Bharati's consort as
Swan-formed. Becomes 21600 breaths in the nostrils;
He is in sun and moon and is in the world.(5)

Five elements as five heads, senses of duty and perception as
Ten shoulders, sin and merit as two feet, ego as waist,
Intellect as belly Hari shining as Vangmanomaya
Lives every day in ten senses, seven elements and
72000 veins and is known as defectless and promoter
of Bharat. (6)

The heavy body with four combined in it is of six Taranga.[1]
Laxmi's consort praised in Purusha Sukta in 16 stanzas
Is Vishnu a support of 64 arts. He is chief among
Bramha, Rudra, and moves in the world. (7)

(Note [1] : The six Tarangas are Asti, Jayate, Parinamate, Vivardhate, Apakshiyate and Vinashyate. (Exists, grows, spreads, grows more, extends and dies.) To explain further - Bramha and other gods have Swarupa, Linga, Aniruddha and Sthooladeha. These are - 1. Asti - Linga, that is, the state earlier than being Sthooladeha; 2. Jayate - being Sthooladeha; 3. Parinamate - crossing baby-hood; 4. Vivardhate - growing into Youth; 5. Apakshiyate - becoming emaciated; 6. Vinashyate - destroying.)

(Basing his arguments on the Vedas, the Geeta and Bhagawata Jagannath Dasa explains life's marvels and those of the Creator. Birth, growth, duties and death and other stages of life are carefully studied and explained for the benefit of readers. The arguments, sometimes, may appear to be abstruse and mathematical with astounding figures. But since bodies of both animate and inanimate things are so complex the study has, naturally, to be complicated. Body's complexity explains the Creator's incomprehensible greatness. Jagannath Dasa wants readers to listen to Hari's story (*Hari Katha*) and to realise even in a small way the supremacy of the all-pervading Hari. He is everywhere yet nowhere; He is seen, yet not seen; He is understood and not understood at all, Jagannath Dasa's main purpose is to teach a common man to humbly bow down to Hari.)

From all lives to Bramha and four bodies
Wise calculate by alphabets Narayan's 5126
The Lord grants health and wealth to those
Who recite, "Om Ghrunih Surya Aditya."[1] (8)

(Note [1] : Hari is the centre of solar circle. (Ghrunih is sun). Therefore people should first pray to Sun. The eight lettered invocation - Om Ghrunih Surya Aditya (eight in Devanagari Script) - has been recommended by Shri Madhvacharya. It is said that Dharma when in forest had no food, obtained the wish-fulfilling cooking pot from sun. Jagannath Dasa recommends that everyone should repeat the invocation.)

In Adi Bhoutik 574 forms, in Adhyatmika 711,
In Adhidaivika 231 forms be worshipped by Brahmins. (9)

Shri Hari resides as Surachi and Sharvarika
With 360 forms in Sankarshana, Pradyumna
Moon and Sun. He is in days and years. Know
His names, He will grant health and wealth. (10)

Hari with 51 alphabets resides everywhere, inside
Outside, in sky; forms Vedas, Grammar and Puranas;
He teaches them simple to understand. (11)

Named Bharabhrut, Hari's 2624 idols
Are spread in world. Meditate on His
24 inanimate and 16 animate forms.
He becomes physically present everywhere. (12)

Like diamond in gold Hari shines in Bramha and others.
Called King of the World, Unequalled, He is 242 forms
In moon and 142 forms in moon crescent. (13)

Praise the Lord realising His 2008 forms and
Pray for blessings. With no respect for elders and
Teachers, what use is it in bathing and telling beads? (14)

Lover of devotees, fear-destroyer, prosperity-incarnate,
Hari resides in all beings in 80725 forms. With
Narasimha form He removes unnatural death. (15)

In fever 27, in Rudra 28, in illness-remover

Narasimha 2827 forms resides Hari. Remember
Him and sins will vanish like melting snow by Sun. (16)

Remember continuously for a month Narasimha's
Auspicious name. Sit with fixed mind, with
Clean mind meditate on the Lord; He will
Remove your sins and grant your wishes. (17)

Four-formed Hari is with 30 forms in Bramha;
With 27 forms in Pradyumna-Vayu; with 25 forms
In Garuda Shesh Rudra; with 18 forms in
Aniruddha - years. Thus in 100 years He
Bears 100 forms to bê sincerely worshipped. (18)

100 years have 36000 days; in body
Are 36000 male veins 36000 female veins
Spread right and left. Remember Hari's
72000 forms in them and worship Him. (19)

In time (past, present, future), in action
In quality and in beings is Laxmi's consort,
Protects all as Time, Action, Quality; as Rudra
Destroys. Again He creates the world. (20)

Like a burning wick showing light banishing darkness
Lotus-eyed Lord removes His devotees' darkness. (21)

Let Hari give any body, birth in any country,
In any world, in any condition animate or inanimate,
Let Him grant knowledge and devotion to remember Hari.
(22)

Vishnu has many forms; meditate on the form you choose;
Have no disbelief; like water spreading in cloth
Hari is spread everywhere. (23)

Crores innumerable worlds are hidden in one part
Of one country, of one small section of body;
Did not Markandeya (a sage) witness Lord's work in the
deluge? (24)

Each form has myriad forms; each such form has many worlds;
Lord has spread in the world undertaking its
Creation, preservation and destruction. Did not
Krishna reveal His Universal form to Arjuna? (25)

Lords's idol appears the same like the picture of nine-women-elephant;[1]
Looks different in different parts. Though different
In different bodies He is nonconcerned;
His body is, indeed, the entire world. (26)

(Note [1] : Nine-women-elephant is like the five-women-horse referred in Stanza 8 of Canto V. The nine women elephant picture shows an elephant outwardly to a casual onlooker. But when he watches the same picture carefully, he sees nine women joining together to form the figure of an elephant. Similarly Shri Hari, to a casual observer, appears to be one figure but in fact, he has many forms.)

Laxmi Narayan's qualities, forms in the world
Are spread like ocean waves. He reveals to the
Wise as creator, destroyer, omnipresent God,
Avatar, world manager. Ignorant people
Witness not His innumerable forms. (27)

Like a string in a necklace, Hari moves
Around in the world every day. Being
Joy incarnate merciful Lord manages the
World in different forms. (28)

Hari is different;[1] there are differences in
Living beings, inanimate things, Living and non-living;
Laxmi, too, is different, But one should praise
Both Laxmi and Narayana. (29)

(Note [1] : Jagannath Dasa reiterates the basic principles of Madhva philosophy of difference or Taratamya.)

What Gods not realised is understood
By Veda-patrons Saraswati and Bharati.
Bramha knows what qualities of Hari
Unknown to them. Only Laxmi understands
The supreme Lord's incomprehensible (to Bramha) qualities. (30)

Laxmi having understood Hari's unending qualities,
Has herself become His ornament, weapon,
Dress and Home. She has become His
Eternal slave to extol His qualities. (31)
Like a boat caught in a deluge circling Laxmi,
Thinking of Lord's unblemished form and qualities
Is fickle because she can touch no shore.
How then, can mortals fully know Hari's greatness? (32)

Devotees that trust Jagannath Vitthal as
Laxmi's home, Lord of the sages, known by wisdom,
Demon-killer, worshipped by Rushis, devotee-lover,
Killer of Madhu demon and protector of world,
Are supported everyday. (33)

Canto VIII

DESIGN OR FORM OF DIVINITY

(Jagannath Dasa continues the idea of God's existence in the world in general and in the body in particular. Bodies of both animate and inanimate things/beings are considered and God's existence in different parts of the body is emphasized. It should be noted that the Dasa, a well-read scholar, has an intimate knowledge of human anatomy. Whether or not one accepts the various names associated with the parts, the reader should realise that the anatomical description of the body would surprise even a methodically trained medical man. References to thousands of veins, to muscles, to minute body parts are the many examples of Jagannath Dasa's scholarly approach.

The present canto is based on the Tantric devices of meditation involving the human body. Each part has a presiding deity and is supervised by the Supreme Being. Here the Dasa describes the divine presence in the body.)

Foot-proud Jayant has the Lord Sumedha.
Vayu in the right toe has Bharabhrut.
From thigh corners to the toes and in joints
Below waist lives Tankitara named God in ten forms. (1)

The forms of Kapila, Charvanga lives in
Finger joints doing many things. Right and left
Sideshave phala and para. Anus and body centre
(generative organs)

Have Bali and Bhaga. Below navel is Mana. (2)

Six-petalled five lotuses exist at navelroot;
Hari is in them as Aniruddha and other forms;
He gives life and makes them perform suitably. (3)

In the six corners of navel is Vayu in whom
Presents god-served Pradyumna. Wearing Kaustubha

And other ornaments He shines and is fearful
To sinners. (4)

Twelve-cornered Solar constellation is joined to
Sushumna vein in belly centre. Hari pacifies
Presiding deitics of 360 days and nights by killing
Demon Nishada. (5)

In the eight-petalled heart-lotus resides Lord
Named Pradesha who shines like Sun. He wears
Many ornaments on head, body and fingers. (6)

Two-petalled lotus is in throat presided by
Prana-god and wife who pray to Hamsa, giving
Food and water He lives as Udana. (7)

In nose are Nasatya and Dasra Ashwini Gods;
Also breath-proud Vayu and Bharati; in them is
Hamsa-formed Dhanwantari. Sun and moon (medical doctor)
Are in two eyes. Laxmi's is as Dadhi and Waman
in them. (8)

In right eye is Pradyumna as Sthambakara; (Pole)
Rama is like a rope; Vayu and other Gods
Are as a calf. (9)

In eyes are sages Vasishta, Vishwamitra and others;
Along with them Hari is worshipped by Rudra and
other gods. (10)

In the eye-shine is Kapila; in the front of right eye
Is the white-coloured, four-armed, eighteen faced
Lord. He grants knowledge and prosperity. (11)

Many gods are in ears; people think that
Ganga is in the right ear are purified. (12)

Indra and Love-god are in mind; Rudra
In ego, in mind and life-force are
Garuda and Shesha. In them is Hari as

Nineteen-faced Taijasa who presents happy dreams. (13)

Taijasa gives knowledge; makes them realise
His greatness; without revealing His true form
Wakes them and leads them to a state of awakening. (14)

Varuna and Matsya are in tongue; in Uvula
Are Upendra and Indra, in throat are Parijanya
And Ardhagarbha. Inside the eyes are Sudhamana
And Wamana; in the forehead are Shiva and
Keshava; in the cheeks are Love-god and
Pradyumna. (15)

In body hair are Vasanta and Trikashuddham;
In mouth Agni and Parashurama; in head Bramha
And Vasudeva; in mind Laxmi and Vishnu;
In stone Parvati and Parameshwara and Narasimha;
Think thus and pray to ward off untimely death. (16)

Vasudeva in the roof of head as Aja, Ananda assumes sixteen forms
Spreads in face, eyes, ears and is involved in
Various activities. One hears, sees and speaks because of him. (17)

Of 72000 veins are 101 veins; these have 101
Forms; Brahmins think Hari residing in these
As Kusha and worship Him. (18)

(In all the stanzas the word "form" is used for idol or "Murti" or "Roopa". God's different forms are manifested in different idols or "Roopa".)

In the previous canto and in the present one the reader will certainly notice many repetitions and ineffective stanzas. There are very few brilliant similes and illustrations for which Jagannath Dasa is famous. As I have said earlier many stanzas are, perhaps, interpolations, and unintentionally prove to be killers of the beauties of Harikatha. Repetitions not only mar the excellences of the poem but also add boredom to the reader. Since nothing conclusive can be indicated here, one has to accept the poem as is available.)

Heavenly river is in twelve veins; holy places in ears;

Padmanabha in twelve forms resides there,
Immersed in Sushumna vein. (19)
Pradyumna resides in Sushumna, Ida and
Pingala veins and reveals as Saraswati, Vayu
And Bramha and makes us perform our duties. (20)

He is called year, season, month, fortnight; He
Is everywhere as Aniruddha in five forms;
The merciful Lord shows Himself in 45
Forms to His devotees. (21)

Hari of five forms has 25 forms and 360 days.
Place your mind firmly in the day-proud Lord
To relieve you of your problems. (22)

Like Ganga Hari flows in day, Muhurta and moment;
Rama moving in His whirlpool of qualities,
Form and duties, is always joyful. (23)

Veda-proud Laxmi not realising Hari's great
Qualities expresses to be His wife always. She
Thinks Hari would accept her plea like a rich man
Helping a beggar. (24)

Wise know that in the differentiation, Laxmi
Excels in qualities from Brahma as much as
Grass from living being. Even such a goddess cannot
Grasp Hari's greatness; what of mortals? (25)

Hari as Vasanaroopa and Rasaroopa resides in
Milk, curds, butter and ghee; Aniruddha is
Found in Bharati, Saraswati, Vayu and Bramha
Known for knowledge, action, desire and strength. (26)

Four formed Hari exists in 8 Vasus, 6 Prajeshwar,
50 Marudganas, 11 Suns, 11 Rudras, 2 Ashwinis,
All Ninety. He is a promoter of Bramha Vayu,
Garuda and Shesha. (27)

In disc He is Hinkara, in conch Pratihara,

In mace Nidhana, in lotus Prastava, in
Caste marks ("nama") Udgeetha; meditate on
Laxmi's consort existing in the five formed weapons. (28)

Body is a chariot, Uma, proud of speech, is a rope.
Rohini Moon in ears reins; Sun and Sanjna
Are horses; Rudra is charioteer; Omkar-promoter
Hari sits in the chariot. (29)

Can Shrutis, limited in words praise the
Limitless qualities? Shruti-Smruti-proud
Bramha, Rudra, Indra and others though
Constantly meditating fail to understand Him.
Only He alone knows His birth, life and end. (30)

Think that Hari exists in wealth, body, house,
Wife and children, and friends; please the good,
The indifferent, the sinful alike and not
Being egotistic be a servant of God. (31)

If you worship god of gods, and be happy
With His meditation, Jagannath Vitthal will
Be merciful and remove all problems. (32)

Canto IX

LIFE STORY

(This canto has been called "Varna Prakriya Sandhi" and "Udatta Anudatta Sandhi". The author discusses the long and the short sounds, the thoughts about living beings and the existence of Shri Hari in each body. The author, as in the previous cantos, devotes many stanzas to the narration of Hari's every-present forms in His creations.)

Hari is 50 alphabets; He in their
Pronunciation, rise and fall of sounds,
Sandhi and Visarga. Only gods on earth
Know how to pronounce, not mortals. (1)

Create interest in Hari, respect for devotees,
Disinterest in pleasure, understand the presence
Of Hari in false philosophers and everyone.
Helping such devotees is by itself worship. (2)

Famous for thirteen forms, with three in
Earth, water and fire and in Vayu presiding
Deity of ten organs. He, revealing to wise,
Accepts all pleasures. (3)

Three important duties are as bodily, regional and timely;
Remember Vayu in 72000 veins and work
Not expecting rewards. Offer your work to Hari. (4)

Krishna, Parashuram, and Hayagriva formed-Lord
Makes us do three duties. Wearing nine
Forms He is in god, man and demon. He accepts
People's worship. (5)

Like fire-cooked rice offered to fire, duties
Hari made us to perform, be offered to Him

With body, speech and mind. Then He will
Accept them to bless. (6)

Horse's hair at tail-end be cut into 100 parts
Each part again cut into 100 parts; He lives
Like an atom in life from Bramha to grass.
He is neither big nor small. (7)

Idol of toe's size, toe's end's size, idol of
Very small, medium and big sizes; such are
The forms of Hari in the world. (8)

The wise call Him Vishwambara, Atma, Prajnya;
He of toe's size occupies heart's centre;
The Universal Lord supports His devotees. (9)

Lord named purusha lives in all beings in their size;
Hrushikesha promotes senses; Turiya-named Hari
Lives twelve cubits above head and 72 thousand veins. (10)

He spreads among living, makes them work
Remaining unconcerned; being served
By Laxmi, Bramha, Vayu He is in the centre of
the world. (11)

Bearing the names of Garuda, Shesha, Rudra
Hari assumes Vayu's form and presides over senses;
With Bramha, Saraswati, Bharati, Vayu
He creates a place in living beings. Other gods have
no place. (12)

Like outer grain chaff protecting the inner, with outer body,
He occupies the inner body.
Laxmi presides over non-living body; till one
Bathes in Viraja river the body clings to His inner
presence. (13)

In the 16 part Aniruddha and Lingadeha
Are two evil elements called Jeevachhadita and
Paramachhadita.

Janardana lives in Lingadeha as "Trivat" to drive out
Demons coming near living being. (14)

Aniruddha body is Rudra and other gods' home,
They still do nothing. But in Sthooladeha
Angered demons and gods mutually fight
And perform good and bad deeds as ordered by Vayu. (15)

In the world even in rain, cold, living beings
Perform duties related to body, country and time.
Bramha and other gods undertake this work
According to three qualities. (16)

Sushumna vein spreads from head-roof to body centre.
It is a thousandth part of end of hair
It is named Vajraka, Arya, Prakashini and Vaidyuti.
The vein extends to north, west, south and east. (17)

In Bramha (Sushumna) vein in heart-centre is a traingular disk.
In this centre resides Sankarshana who destroys
Evil. Merciful Hari is in Vayu-form and intelligence incarnate. (18)

In the centre of Sushumna vein below heart-lotus
Resides Moolesh-named Hari. Here living being
Is Lingadeha and Aniruddha while Rudra
And other gods are in the eight-petalled lotus. (19)

In the eight-petalled lotus lives Hamsa-named Hari
Revolving like potter's wheel. Receives eight
Direction-gods (Ashtadikpalaka) service and blesses them. (20)

Indra's brother Upendra, Parashurama, Rama
Janardana, Matsya, Hayavadana, Shri Kapila,
Narasimha are the eight forms that make
People happy and live in heart-lotus. (21)

Hari lives in the eastern-petal which is Indra's abode,

He makes living beings happy and meritorious.
If Agni comes to live there, sleep, idleness, thirst are gone;
Surya's son Yama coming there, anger and shouting
If Hari comes to Nirutipetal [1] beings commit sins. (22)

(Note [1] : This has reference to the heart considered to be eight-petalled lotus. God and other presiding deities live from time to time in the eight petals. They influence man's behaviour when they are powerfully residing in each petal. This stanza elaborates the above idea.)

Humour and wit generate with Hari reaching Varuna's
petal in west;
Reaching Vayu's petal in Vayavya (north-east) creates
travelling;
Coming Moon and Kuberas' petal in north generates religious
feeling;
Reaching Hara's petal in Ishanya (west-south) creates charity
in giving cow, daughter, land and riches. (23)

Hari reaching the centre of heart-lotus creates
Renunciation; reaching the middle flower produces dreams;
Reaching Lingbody generates sleep; coming to
Petals produces awakening; wearing Sudarshana
And other weapons Hari always moving generates
intelligence. (24)

Hamsa-named, Hari, master of Sutra-named
Prana, a promoter of Gayatri, exists in our body;
Ignorantly with wife and children we go on
Pilgrimage and gloat over it. (25)

Narasimha lives in 16 parts in Linga Body;
In Aniruddha body He is Shantapati; in
Sthoolbody He is Pradyumna. (26)

In the body are skin-sense covering skin, blood, fat, pus and
bones;
49 Marudgunas exist there. Hari, promoter of SamaVeda,
Named Nidhana, Hinkara, lives in 49 forms and
7 elements. (27)

Unconcerned Hari resides in 7 elements in and
Out food pipes and like a burning iron He
Shines and offers suitable blessings. As Taijasa,
Prajna and Vishwa He induces dream,
Awakening and deep sleep. (28)

In our fingers and toes is Majja (an element);
With 1080 forms Hari enjoys there according
to the wise. (29)

Like a caterpillar turning into a butterfly
A person thinking of Hari will soon cross
The worldly ocean. (30)

Jagannath Vitthal makes devotees realise Lord's
Forms in body and meditate on them
To visualise His presence. (31)

Canto X

PRESENCE EVERYWHERE

(This canto is called "Sarvasamarpana Sandhi" by some publishers. It is "Sarva Pratika Sandhi", a canto that narrates the presence of Shri Hari everywhere.

Jagannath Dasa continues the same argument that Hari is all-pervasive and manifests Himself in all bodies and in different forms. It is the duty of the devotee to find out how he can visualize God and how he can obtain His grace.)

How will the Supreme Lord who is served
By Bramha and other gods and by
His devotees destroy anyone? Will His
Servants ever face defeat? (1)

Devotees who worship Hari's feet with
Fixed eleven sense-mind get protection
From nine planets, their patron-gods
By driving away physical and mental illnesses. (2)

On earth water in cow-foot-print is holy;
Trees, mountains and land are pilgrim spots;
All living beings Hari's reflections;
The food they eat is Lord's blessing;
The path they traverse is dance;
Thus consider Yogis. (3)

To a devotee who worships Hari
Every country is a holy place,
Every time is auspicious,
Everyone deserves charity in three worlds;
All speech is incantation,
All work is Lord's worship. (4)

Patrons (gods) of rivulet, tank, well (stepped) and
Lakes exist in our body cavities; think that
Akasha-Ganga and other rivers flow in our 72000 veins. (5)

The wise are gods who think that Hari in Vayu-form
Shines everyday in our body in 30072000 forms;
Their bodies are holy pilgrim spots and their worship Hari's
worship. (6)

Wise who bathe anywhere offering water as
Lord's bath have benefits of bathing in Ganga.
Ignorant of this will obtain nothing though they
Bathe in Ganga. (7)

Rivers join and pour together into sea;
Wise likewise do their duties, good and bad;
All duties are abandoned when meditating on God. (8)

Under Hari's orders Bramha, Rudra and other gods
Reside in Kali and other wickeds and perform
Duties; deeds are offered to Hari and blessed. (9)

Do they (Bramha and others) what duties they want;
Live they where they want; worship they what form
They want, with Hari's mercy sin touches them not. (10)

Wife enjoys with husband, bears children
Still she is senses-controlled; listening to Hari's
Life-story will never be polluted by sins. (11)

If one swims against current to show adventure,
He will drown; likewise not caring for Hari's
Ordained duties if one worships others
He will seek nothing but misery. (12)

Egoiotistic man's daily rituals of bath, prayer
Will be snatched by demons; Srinivasa will
Receive them not; they will be useless like
Wild elephant eating a ripe sour fruit. (13)

What if one visits all pilgrim centres, offers
Food discriminatingly, cleansing body and
Offers prayers; all a waste if Hari's omnipresence is not
realised. (14)

What good is got if one bathes in water punishing his body
When he fixes not his mind on Shri Hari? (15)

What use is there if one not conquering his
Lust, anger, ego and pride reads Vedas, Shastras
Puranas and holy stories; he may avoid things
Prohibited, control his breath? (16)

What good if one listens to, reads, speaks, sings everyday.
If he remembers not Srinivasa's life and works
And meditates on Him not? (17)

I have written not this poem as intellectual exercise,
Nor is this just poetry; I have learned from
The wise no religious rules. I have written
Just what Guru Madhvacharya's master Shri Hari
Standing in me has dictated. Wise should
Listen to this ignoring its defects. (18)

(After Jagannath Dasa wrote nine cantos on many aspects of Shri Hari's province he again humbly justifies what he has written. It is no ego, no pride that he has written a great poem. Though a renowned scholar Jagannath Dasa admits right in the beginning that he has learned everything, from the wise. Finally, *Harikatha* is no ordinary poetic exercise; it is a flow of poetry from the Guru's master, Shri Hari.

A reader wonders how this stanza came suddenly in the tenth canto. The present stanza deals with the author's humility and should, like other stanzas of similar nature, have gone into the first canto. But one has to realise that Canto X deals with the real path to god-realization. Many stanzas deal with shedding ego and becoming humble. So, a stanza about the author's humble gratitude to Shri Hari is not out of place.)

Will a toothless person understand the sweetness of
sugarcane juice?
Only those who devotedly drink Hari's feet-lotus-honey
Will enjoy *Harikatha*; not those who are
Proud of their wealth and youth. (19)

The poem will be an unsolvable riddle to those ignorant
Of Hari's feet. Devotees (Bhagawatas) enjoying
Hari's unpolluted qualities will obtain knowledge
And happiness. (20)

This book contains great tenets; Brahmins need listen respectfully;
The book should not be read to criminals,
Foods, intellect-proud, stupids having no knowledge of
Preceptor's teaching and non-connoisseurs.
It be read with pleasure to those, who, like
Honey-bee, are fixed on Hari's feet-lotus. (21)

(Jagannath Dasa explains the great qualities of *Harikatha.* It is not an ordinary poem titillating people's poetical nerves but a great religio-philosophical work. It is fit to be read by people and to people, who are initiated into the appreciation stage. Not everyone who can read can understand the poem. Since the poem is *Harikatha* it has to be revered and treated with care. Jagannath Dasa makes a claim for *Harikatha* not out of ego but out of respect for Hari. Since Hari is venerable, His story told out of no artificiality or arrogance is highly revered.)

This is no worldly news; it is Vaikuntha
Master's story. How can the sinful read it?
They are deep in the world; they know not
His greatness. A honey-bee alone reaches
Red lotus; what can a frog know? Thus
Only Hari devotees, none else, can appreciate this. (22)

You are non-asking (favours), wish-fulfilling;
Repository of shining qualities, fame not easily comprehensible,
Free from old age, death; free from illness; superior
To the wise Bramha and others; soul of universe;
Merciful, bright as sun, worshipped by Laxmi,
King of gods, victory to you. (23)

Fish, tortoise, bearing mountain Mandara.
Earth-saving Varaha, Narasimha, Vamana,
Parashurama, Sita's Consort, Krishna, Buddha,
Kalki, victory to you Shri Hari. (24)

Hari has a pleasing person, whose feet are worshipped
By Bramha; He is supreme, offering good rewards,
Resides firmly in Madhvacharya; indestructible,
Saved cowherds by swallowing forest fire; Such
Jagannath Vitthal will certainly protect His devotees. (25)

Canto XI

METHOD OF MEDITATION

(This canto is called "Dhyanakriya Sandhi" or "Sthavara Jangama Sandhi" by many publishers. Jagannath Dasa describes the methods of Hari-meditation; also points out body formation, thoughts about veins, work of senses, procedures of worshipping God and also performing Puja of idols. Idol worship is justified by many arguments. One has to be fully engrossed in the idea that Shri Hari is the master, director, organiser of all actions in the world; we should worship Him without expecting any reward because all our actions should be dedicated to Him.

Jagannath Dasa repeats the idea already enunciated in the earlier cantos. He emphasizes certain more aspects of the omnipresence of Shri Hari.)

Will thorns and sand prick a person
Wearing foot-wear? Likewise a person
Constantly meditating on Hari will
Conquer all sins in the way of release. (1)

Like a lamp before god one has to worship
Hari not expecting any worldly benefits;
Enjoy what He has offered, think everything
From wife, children to body and life to His. (2)

Life is not free, poor, conditioned by rules,
Ignorant, miserable, impotent, small bodied.
Hari alone is its master. Praise Him as
Omnipotent, joy-incarnate, omnipresent,
Saluted by Bramha Rudra and others. (3)

Eight universal forms multiplied by nine
Will be seventytwo; think that in each is a
Thousand with 72000 and in 3200 veins is Hari; thus
Spoke Bhishma to Dharma in Shanti Parva. (4)

Eight elements have eight universal forms
To remove devotees' miseries. Like brothers
Hari saves His worshippers to lead to goodness;
Wicked are left to themselves. (5)

Defectless, joyful Hari existing in Indra and
Others enjoys all pleasures and makes others
Do it. Ignorant of this if one thinks of himself
As doer, he will reach hell and is reborn. (6)

Hari is in four forms as Suruchi, Ruchira,
Sugandha, Suchi in six juices, sweet, bitter,
Salty, Sour, hot and harsh. And He resides
Two forms in twelve such as Shri, Earth,
Durga; in Vayu with 72000 and in veins
With 72000 forms. He is the doer. (7)

One who worships Hari as omnipresent
Finds his sins changed to merit; not
Meditating on Him your bath, beads, sacrifice,
Charity in clothes, elephant, horse and land
Are a waste. (8)

Hari exists in desired things as Shipivishta,
Enjoys them and makes others get them; as
Rasamaya He resides in food canal, generates strength
Makes people happy without showing Himself. (9)

As Karana He lives in sense organs promoting
Sense and physical activities; in all three
Qualified things without revealing His presence
He exists and fools people. (10)

As Dravya deathless Hari resides in five
Elements and related qualities; He is called
Satkriya for action, Stutya for being in bodies,
Karaka and Sevya Sevaka; He exists like
Fire hidden in wood. (11)

Vayu lives as Shuchi in mind; Hari,

Inside Vayu, exists as Shuchi Shat and Hota.
As Hrushikesha and Vamana Hari offers
Pleasure to all people. (12)

Promoter and promotable Hari exists impartially in
Different forms; He invisibly does all duties
And playfully enjoys them. (13)

(Again there is a good deal of repetition here. The same ideas are often expressed in identical expressions. It is very evident that the repetition cannot be the work of Jagannath Dasa. The translator strongly feels that a pseudo author must have added a number of stanzas of his own making to Harikatha in order to obtain respectability, length of the poem and credence to his writing. A masterful writer like Jagannath Dasa would shun any repetition and any inferior writing.)

Be firm that Hari makes us to all duties;
Merit and sin, joy, anger, gain and loss,
Joy and sorrow, all dualities of life be offered to Hari
And Hari remembered in hell, on land and in heaven. (14)

A boy does something purposelessly and
Ignorant of result; he enjoys it; knowingly,
One should consider Hari as the doer;
Not caring for rules of rituals he should
Meditate on the Lord. (15)

Forget gain, loss, victory or defeat, bear them,
Obtain Srinivasa's blessings. Knowledge-repository,
Merciful Hari will protect His devotees. (16)

God existing among all, not revealing, accepts
All pleasures. Sinless Hari through people does duties. (17)

Hari is in birds, beasts, men, water animals,
Ghosts, dead bodies, demons and makes them do
Their work. Friend of Bhima, Lord of Lords, Hari
Is unattainable except by thought. (18)

Father and son of the same Gotra perform
Sandhya,[1] yet they have different names.
Indira's master living in body makes them do

Their duties. (19)

Note [1] : Sandhya or Sandhya Vandana is worship of dawn and dusk. All men after their thread ceremony perform the worship by offering water and uttering Gayatri incantation. Sandhya is considered to be a very important ritual for people.)

Rusted iron is cleaned by fire; rice is pounded
And separated from chaff; devotionally if one says
"Vitthal" He will destroy all sins, burn body,
Take him to His abode. (20)

Like water animals that move in water freely
Bramha Rudra and others roam around in Him. (21)

Vasudev exists inside and outside bodies
Assuming their form is recognised by suitable names.
One who thinks thus is fit for release. (22)

Realise the enjoyable and non-enjoyable;
Offer your services to both deserving and otherwise;
Lord is among both; unattached to riches and
Poverty, devote self to Hari. (23)

One should offer to Hari flowers that grow on land,
Water, mountain, basil and other worship materials
For Him; wise call this worship "Vyatireka". (24)

Not differentiating among merit, form, work think
Of Hari; He will accept your worship; merciful
Lord removing sorrows gives you peace.
This is "Anwaya" worship. (25)

Understand Vyatireka and Anwaya worship,
Bow down to Hari; He will accept them,
Move you away from life, death and birth
And place you near Bramha and others. (26)

Hari has two forms, inanimate and animate;
Animate are male, female; inanimate are
Ahita and Sahajachala; meditate on
Five and three types of forms. (27)

Bramha, Vayu, Garuda, Rudra, Indra, Manmath (Love God)
And others are not visible in male body
But worship body-patron Aniruddha-formed
Narayana and are happy. (28)

Laxmi, Saraswati, Bharati, Sauparni, Varuni
Parvati are patrons of female body; they
Enjoy worshipping day and night red-yellow
Coloured Sankarshana and Aniruddha forms. (29)

In five-metal idol resides Tanki named Hari;
In the idol worshipped by all are Parashurama,
Fire, Vayu and other gods. They grant worshippers
Four-fold blessings if offered basil, sandal,
Coloured rice, fruits, flowers and lamp. (30)

Mountain-patron gods worship Vasudeva in
The idols and Saligram; such omnipresent
Lord be worshipped as female, male, Ahita
And Sahajachala, to cross the ocean of world. (31)

One who doesn't realise Jagannath Vitthal
As spreading everywhere in animate and
Inanimate things achieves nothing even
when he goes on a pilgrimage; what if he
Bathes in holy rivers, performs sacrifices
And offers charity. (32)

Canto XII

CONCERNING VEINS

(Body contains a number of veins which are a great help to keep the body working. The entire life system depends on millions of nerves. Hari is spread in the system and is responsible for its proper functioning. Jagannath Dasa tells this in a general way in the earlier cantos. He points out the names of presiding gods and connects the system to Shri Hari.

As the translator has mentioned earlier Jagannath Dasa is a voracious reader and astounding scholar. His knowledge of the world is easily witnessed in the many references he makes to different aspects of life. His scholarship does not limit itself to general aspects of life but to a detailed study of human anatomy and physical capacities. In everything he attaches his findings to the existence of Shri Hari. *Harikatha* is Lord's story. It is by His Grace that the world functions; it is by His knowledge every object in the world, outside the world act. Action appears to be ours but one has to realise who the doer is. The promoter is Shri Hari; He is the motive force and moves everything in His creation.)

Vasudeva accepting Vayudeva's services
Lives in 36000 body-veins alongwith Shridevi and Bhudevi,
Enjoy yourself by praying to Hari's beautiful idol. (1)

In feet are 12000 veins, in body-centre 14000,
In shoulders 4000, in head 6000; remember
36000 veins. One year has 360 days and 360 nights,
One hundred years has 36000 days and 36000 nights. (2)

Defectless; great and merciful Vasudeva named Brahati
Assumes male-female forms (72000) and
Lives in 72000 veins; He is worshipped by
Gods and protects all living beings. (3)

100 years have 36000 days; 36000 veins are in body;

Thinking of Brahati-named patron, if one
Worships one wise man a day, it will be one couple a week;
He obtains so much merit. (4)

24 tenets, their patrons Bramha and others
Exist in every vein; enjoy watching Hari
Who is eternal and protects all 14 worlds. (5)

Sarvottama, ever-auspicious Hari resides sin
72000 veins assuming 3456000 forms and
With Laxmi bears the welfare of all. (6)

Hari lives in all like a thread of a necklace.
The Supreme Lord exists in heavy bodies
But appears to be light. (7)

Sushumna veins and other vein-mass are
Below navel between Vrukshala and seat; it is Tundi;
Moolesha-named Hari is worshipped. (8)

Let wise know that Ganga and other holy
Rivers are in 72000 veins; not revealing
This to the ignorant, devotees bathe in the rivers. (9)

Bramha, Vayu and Saraswati live in the right veins;
Garuda, Shesha, Rudra, Krishna's six wives,
Varuni, Indra and Love-god live in the left. (10)

Moving with the patron-gods Hari makes
People perform according to their merit and
Blesses them; demons don't do good deeds;
Those even He takes Himself. (11)

From "Tundi" to head only Bramha vein spreads;
Bramha and Vayu reside there; it has ten branches.
Eleven veins are connected with eleven senses;
It's a home of sun, moon, sea-god, Ashwinis. (12)

From navel-bottom spreads on straight vein
Upto mid-back; called Sushumna is a

Residence of Vayu who prevents demons from entering. (13)
The veins contain Narayana's form called "Ekatma"
Spread in 72000 forms; with Laxmi and her
Forms He protects the world day and night. (14)

Blind man can't enjoy, waxing moon-rays.
Likewise except for Hari's devotees this poem
On Hari will have no use. (15)

Veins have spread in body; Indra and other
Gods residing in them threaten demons and
Worship Hari by "Sandhata" name. (16)

Residing by those forms of water, land and sky animals
Hari not revealing Himself makes them work
He himself obtains no rewards. (17)

Think thus, see not the wicked, show not
Pride before the wise. More around like a
Wild elephant caring not for rain, sun,
Hunger, thirst, success or defeat, abuses of the unworthy. (18)

Believe that all beings in forest or town work
For Hari; meditate on Him and offer all your services. (19)

Hari existed in world as dog, pig and had
Many names in incarnations. He remains
In them unseen and is worshipped by all. (20)

Devotees should think their worship to be Hari's;
Being true this can't be doubted except by the ignorant;
What use if outside duties are performed? (21)

Hari remains in enjoyables and enjoyers and becoming enjoyer
And enjoyed He grants blessings to both
The deserving and the non-deserving. He
Grants devotees devotion and knowledge,
Hatred for Hari to haters. (22)

Vamana remains in 14 worlds and roams

As a mendicant; Hamsa-named Hari
Destroys mirage-like world and as "Nishe-
Chaka" grants people's desires. (23)

He gives food, eats, is full of food, offers food
To Bramha and others; these He does as
Aniruddha; merciful Lord creates and protects world. (24)

Patron of Gayatri, King of gods, resident of Vaikuntha,
Father of Ganga, Trivikrama, devotee favourite,
Blue-coloured, joy-incarnate Lord will protect His
devotees. (25)

Water mixed with salt tastes salty, can one
Separate salt from it? Hari is spread all over
Among living beings. Are there many who
Know Him? (26)

Since He is omnipresent the world-worried
Should praise Him. He will pardon them
And break their birth-death cycle. (27)

Praise Hari in a myriad way, offer them to Him,
He found everywhere grants you wisdom and prosperity. (28)

(The reader will again notice a number of identical stanzas; repetition is spread throughout the poem. Perhaps, like Hari who is spread all over the world, repetition, certainly the work of a hackwriter, negatives the extraordinary beauty of the poem. A good editor should cut off repetitions and restore to *Harikatha* its pristine beauty and glory.)

Hari is defectless, many forms incarnate ("Avatar")
Protector of three worlds, primeval being,
Praised by Indra and others, lying on Shesha,
Loved by Vibhishana,[1] Arjuna's friend; such
Hari will serve the good. (29)

(Note [1] : Vibhishana was Ravana's brother. He constantly advised his brother to release Sita, respect Rama and respect a decent life. But Ravana did not listen to him. When he was killed Vibhishana was made King of Lanka.)

His lotus-feet are served by Sridevi, Bhudevi;

Full in all respects, achieved only by good devotion;
Worshipped by Bramha, Vayu, Garuda, Shesha, Rudra;
Vamana, Rama, a medicine for world-disease;
Oh, Lord, protect me; thus should a devotee
Praise the merciful. (30)

Being in gods and demons He makes them work;
Hari free from birth and death appears to be born with us;
Like a wealth guarding serpent He lives in us
To protect us always. (31)

As the sun rises tree-shades collect
Near trunk; with sunset they disappear;
Likewise hidden Hari with three worlds
Concealed in Himself reveals them only to a few. (32)

Hari worshipped by Laxmi is born at will;
Joy in form, gold coloured, Garuda-rider,
Fear remover, bright like unlimited suns cool like
Many moons, defectless Hari will grant
Blessings to devotees who worship Him. (33)

Some people learned from the wise the sacrifices
For morning, noon and evening; offered them
To gods of the time Rudra, Aditya, Vayu and
Husbands of Jaya and Mayadevi; they are
Sankarshana and Vasudeva in form. Sacrificing
In their name devotees are happy. (34)

In Ashtava for 24 years is Pradyumna, for 44
Years in Rudra is Sankarshana, then for 48
Years in Sun Shetashariri, Vasudeva exists
As Maya's consort. (35)

Thus in 116 years in 116 forms in Vasu, Rudra
Aditya roams Hari with His wives; devotees
That Worship sincerely live with no fear or problem. (36)

Patrons of day and night have 83520 forms (116 years)
Lord in Vayu, Bharati is invisible and called

Hinkara, Nidhana and Prathama and removes
All adversities. (37)

If purposely an expensive silk cloth is dipped
In mud will mud defile it? Likewise Hari
Exists in all beings undefiled. He is untouched
By wordly qualities. (38)

Shining like hundred suns, Laxmi's consort,
Friend of gods, Hari exists in the world.
He is a friend of all beings. (39)

Hari exists in all beings in each form
And shape. Like sky He is spread everywhere.
Offers blessings not expecting any reward. (40)

Served by Laxmi-Bramha and others
Hari lives in all beings inside and outside
They are in Him; deathless Lord keeps them well
protected. (41)

In one month are 648000 breaths; in 116 years
Will be 648000 x 116 ; if one prays as many
Breaths, Hari will be pleased with him as He
Was with Sudama. (42)

Vasudeva residing in our body makes us
Breathe in a year 7776000 times; merciful
Lord spreading Himself in 14 worlds is
A friend of all. (43)

Vayu residing in three type beings in
Four forms breaths prayers each day 86400 times;
How can I extol the mountain of kindness
Rama has for him? (44)

Laxmi's consort Jagannath Vitthal has made
Me speak; wise need listen to me; if the
Learned treat it defective mine no fault;
Only the wise realise the problem. (45)

Canto XIII

PRAYERS

(The canto in Kannada is "Nama Smarane", remembering Hari's name. This canto is, perhaps, the essence of Harikatha and is charged with devotion. How is God to be prasied, how should a devotee qualify to release himself from worldly sorrows and how a devotee can understand Hari, are thoroughly discussed in the canto. Jagannath Dasa points out what a devotee should eat, what he should make to realise God-head. In his telling, simple poetic style the Dasa illustrates by daily-life examples, how simple it is to please Shri Hari. He shouts, *Sulabha no Hari* (Hari is easy to please) and requests the suffering human beings to utter Hari's name and to lead a pious life. After reading earlier canto of the veins and body parts and of the mind-boggling figures, the reader finds this canto a total relief from boredom. Jagannath Dasa is a master of simplicity amd knows how to convey intricate philosophy in simple language.)

Remember Devaki's son when playing with children,
When pleasantly talking with wife,
When in hiccoups or yawning; such person
Cannot be found by Death's servants. (1)

When seeing a flowing river, while tearing
A twin new cloth or a banana dinner leaf,
Joyfully or angrily opening one's mouth
He should say "Hari, Hari"; like fire in cotton
All sins will be burnt. (2)

While sleeping, getting up, talking at home,
While working, bathing, eating if one
Remembers Hari's suitable name, He
Will always be with him. (3)

Let him belong to any caste

Let him reside in any country
Let him do what he wants; he should
Know omnipresent Hari and worship Him.
How can sins touch a wise man? (4)

Who floats in Vasudeva's sea of glory
Can easily cross world's sea of sorrow.
One who not finding devotion wallows
In wordly affairs and suffers greatly. (5)

All sense and function organs act; work
So done belongs to Shriniwasa.
What good is there if one doesn't realise
But observes silence, bath, counting beads,
And Lord's prayers, all done mechanically? (6)

Will sins affect one who lives on Ganga-bank?
Is there fear of snakes in Garuda's home? Think Hari to be
The doer, not life, and free self from sins. (7)

Say not "I have done all good and bad";
You are condemned. "Mine are bad deeds,
Lord does good", says the ordinary man.
(middle-level)
"It's Hari who does good and bad through me",
Says the best man and lives happily. (8)

Such people, are equal to gods; serve them
It is Hari's worship; they assume Lord's form
And bless people like Hari Himself. (9)

I'm my body; wife, children, property are all mine;
Ganga and others are holy places; Lord's worship
Is praying to metal idol; the wise are my equals;
Speaking thus he becomes a stupid ass. (10)

Fire, Parvati and Ishwar, Sun, moon, stars
Earth, Ganga, holy places, wind, sky, mind
Eleven-organ patrons and wise all worship.
Should they pray with no mind, prayer is worthless. (11)

Will not fire touched intentionally or not burn?
Likewise saluting devotees of Hari will
Burn all sins. (12)

Make friends with the wise; don't praise
The wicked being enamoured of worldly pleasures.
Forget everything else, meditate on Hari in His
Varied forms and names. (13)

Hari lives in all creatures and does work;
Ignoring this none should arrogate power to himself
And be condemned. Hari is the independent doer. (14)

Purifying Ganga has water animals. Do they
Know Ganga's greatness? Though blessed by
Merciful God Bramha, Vayu, Garuda, Rudra
Know not Hari's infinite forms. (15)

Existing in heart-lotus of all Laxmi's consort makes
Living beings three-quality controlled. Making
Them involved in worldly pleasures Hari sees
How beings revolve aimlessly around like potter's
wheel. (16)

He grants heavenly bliss to people who study Vedas,
Avoid prohibited things, perform good deeds.
Men realise a mixture of joy and sorrow.
Demons only suffer mentally in hell. (17)

Non-idol worshippers by His Grace reach salvation;
Veda-reading alone doesn't get Him;
Being beyond three qualities, Hari grants
Sorrow and joy in three worlds. Turns people
To move in heaven, earth and hell to suit their action. (18)

Hari residing though in three-typed lives is immune to
sorrows;
Purest of the pure, superior to Rama and Bramha
Is an ocean of joy. Making the world His body

He lives in different forms from Rama to the lowest. (19)
Roam around like a wild elephant believing
That Hari does everything, not he; Vayu-respected Hari
Will leave you not for a minute. (20)

Not physically suffering after performing many duties,
Fix Hari in your heart-lotus. Worship Him. Without
Such realization He will not accept fruits, flowers,
Water, basil offered to Him. (21)

On earth is Narayana, Vasudeva in water, in fire Sankarshana,
In wind Pradyumna, in sky Aniruddha; assuming
Thus five forms, called by different names, He protects. (22)

In cloud Narayana is called Megha; in water called
Vasudeva; in lightening and thunder called Sankarshana;
In rain Aniruddha called Varsha. (23)

(Even though the canto is directly narrated and very well written, it still has a couple of repetitive, inane stanzas. They are again reminiscent of interpolations.)

People involve in house, wife, children and wealth;
Not discriminating the good and the bad
Indulge in eating, sex, sleep and forget their
Heart-lotus Lord; they just suffer in the world. (24)

Accompanied by Bramha, Garuda, Shesha, Rudra
He lives in forest as Goja, Adrija. Rearing
Through moon birds, beasts, and snakes He lives
In different forms and protects them. (25)

Greatly honoured Narasimha controls in forest;
On land as Vamana, on mountains Keshava,
In sky Trivikrama, in water Matsya Hari stays
To save His devotees. (26)

Six forms as Karana, Antaryami, Sthool,
Avatara, Vyapta, Ansha are in juices called
Sara, Shubha, Pravivikta, Anand, Sthool, Nissar.

Preach these forms to the learned and live happily. (27)
Clean reflected moon is tried to be eaten
By water animals; likewise not realising the juices
Accepted by Krishna, we proudly pray and ask for worldly pleasures. (28)

Existing in gods, Rushis, Gandharva, ancestors,
Kings, men, demons, cows, goats, donkey, sheep
Hari accepts what they eat. He offers juices to
suit them. (29)

(The present stanza clearly emphasizes the presence of God everywhere. There is no distinction among animals and gods. Hari resides in each one of them, digests their food and offers them support to suit their capacities. The universality of God is a vital point never to be forgotten by anyone.

Jagannath Dasa points out Hari's supremacy and omnipresence. His story, therefore, has necessarily to be fantastic.)

Give up wickedness, leave worldly talk, consider
Gold, coconut shell, tile to be all same; think
Hari to be supreme, He residing in all
Performs all actions. (30)

People punish if insulted; devotees may
Say, "You killer of maternal uncle, adulterer,
Butter-thief". Yet He punishes you not. (31)

Harikathamrutasara be listened to by the good;
Preach it not to the jealous, low, unworthy. This is
For those who devotionally read Lord's story
And delve deep into its meaning. (32)

Whatever is offered by Hari be accepted with pleasure;
Jagannath Vitthal, great friend, always
Pleasureful will take you across wordly sorrows. (33)

Canto XIV

THOUGHTS ON ANCESTORS

(This canto is called "Sarva Jeevana Kalpa Sandhi". For our physical body two ancestors are responsible. One is Sthira and another Asthira. The canto deals with Hari residing in ancestors and the ways of worshipping them. One has to perform yearly Shraddhas, the seven-food ceremony, and other relevant areas of ancestor worship.)

Krutidevi's consort, Pradyumna in 8 Vasus
In three types of egos is to be enjoyed in 24 forms;
In 11 Rudras Jayapati Sankarshana in 33 forms is the enjoyer. (1)

Mayapati Vasudeva exists in sun and three type ancestors
As Kala in 36 forms; in Vasugana, Pitrugana,
Rudragana and Adityagana Aniruddha
Becomes the doer, the action, and work and
Is known by different names. (2)

Independent Narayana in 8 Vasus in 24 forms,
In 11 Rudras in 33 forms, in 12 suns in 36 forms,
Becomes doer, action, work and called Shannavati;
He accepts devotees' service and grants blessings. (3)

Like cloth Laxmi's consort lives in five forms
As Vasugana, Rudragana, Suryagana and people who work;
Centred in Madhva He blesses people
Who always meditate on Him. (4)

People who for parental love abandon improper action
And do legitimate things will enjoy health,
Fame and all worldly pleasures. (5)

Three-formed Janardana resides in Vasu Rudra,

Adityagana, Pradyumna, Sankarshana, Bramha and others;
Remembering this, worship Garuda-Rider in His 96 forms.
(6)

To ward off obstacles coming in ancestor-worship
Janardana, in 3555 forms, lives in the doer
And the receiver; called by each name Hari
Supports all. (7)

One should pray saying "Victory to Jayakanta,
Sankarshana, Dattatraya, Kapil, Mahidasa,
Bhaktapriya, Primeval Being, Poornanandamaya,
Jnanaswarupa, Hayavadana, Hari, Hamsa,
Stranger that three-world beings, supporter of world,
Free of pollution, have mercy on me." (8)

Shannavati with 96 forms, adored by Laxmi,
Ocean of mercy, a boat to Brahmins to
Cross the ocean of worldly matters, is named
Shannavati who accepts Shraddhas offered. (9)

He gives body, doesn't He offer food?
Shri Hari, worshipped by gods, auspicious,
Mine of good qualities, granter of this-world-
And-Other-World pleasures, bore the mountain
On back and killed demons. (10)

Worshipped by the wise, respected Maya's consort, Vasudeva,
Called Swaha by Bramha and other gods
Makes all happy. Loved by all, Sankarshana
Named Swaha is food. As Pradyumna and
Aniruddha in all grass and grain that grows
He is food to men and animals. Worshippers
Are ferried the impassable ocean of wordly
Miseries. Hari, as food, offers release from the world.
(11,12)

Devotionally offer your actions, good and bad,
Done physically and mentally, to Narayana.
Merciful Lord will accept them and support. (13)

Wise tell of seven types of food. Remembering
Aniruddha forms, say that Laxmi's consort is
The enjoyer, food, food procurer, all Himself. (14)

Realising the 7 food, offer it as sacrifice
Everyday to Govinda. Indira's husband will accept it,
Grant release from miseries. (15)

Like one desiring to conquer world by a needle, ignorant
People in the world don't worship Lord's Lotus-feet,
They suffer not obtaining Dharma, Artha, Kama. (16)

Krishna Himself lives near beings; unseen He
Acts and makes them act; pure devotees get
All happiness; how can I describe His glory? (17)

Laxmi's consort resides in Vaikuntha, in Om, in
Animate, inanimate, in Bramha and others; He is
Known as Moolarupa, Karanarupa and Ansharupa.
Like ghee in milk He is spread in three worlds. (18)

Merciful Lord pleases gods, punishes demons,
Is born in three ages with His people to protect religion;
He assumes human form to beguile people. (19)

Hari as Karana exists in 24 tenets
Assuming different names and forms, creates three worlds;
He reveals Himself as Karya in Saligram. (20)

Hari as Ansha resides in all beings,
In bodies, in senses; enjoying worldly pleasures
Krishna grants men pleasure and demons sorrow. (21)

With no pilgrimages, suffering bodily pain
For worldly pleasures, worship Hari who, as
Bramha, Earth, Water, Fire, Vayu and Sky, is the
chief resort. (22)

There are in the world destructible and indestructible;

Among the destructible are freed and non-freed;
Of the non-freed are those born and not born;
The inanimate and Om are Mahatkal and Anukal;
Hari included will be there; remember the five
differences. (23)

Difference in life and life; nonliving and nonliving;
Life and non-living; Hari is different from all;
Realising the five differences in body, reach
The Lord's abode. (24)

In the beginning are Kshara (destructible) and Akshara
(indestructible) in Rama Madhusudan;
In Kshara are Prakriti, Om, and Kala;
Know the difference from grass to beings;
Teach not the undeserving but meditate yourself on Him.
(25)

From one light will be many to brighten shops and houses
to reveal things;
Hari spreads everywhere in different forms and names
To reveal His greatness. (26)

Rainbow is sun's reflection; three worlds are Hari's;
If Hari's auspicious forms are visualised
Everywhere, Narasimha appears in one's heart. (27)

If white unburnable cloth is dipped in chemical
And dropped in fire, it will burn not; only
Fire will spread. Likewise people immersed in
Rama-devotion-chemical are safe from destruction
By mountains of sins though existing in the world. (28)

Like all rivers joining the sea after flowing separately,
Rama and other three-quality patrons are
Totally immersed in Shri Hari. (29)

Is sun at fault because an owl cannot bear the shine?
This poem with Jagannath's association is
To be enjoyed; what good if fools condemn?

The wise will obtain pleasure reading it. (30)
In the world of inanimate and animate
Jagannath Vitthal in Guru Madhva spreads
Everywhere and creates love for worldly pleasures
To fool demons. He is fearless, always joyful,
Unimpeachable, and free from worldly defects. (31)

Canto XV

RELATED TO BREATHING

(All animals and even trees breathe. Every moment breathing continues and stops only when animals and trees die. The breathing process continues throughout life.

Jagannath Dasa believes that Vayu (Madhvacharya Guru) breathes the name of Hari and repeats the action for the well-being of all. Vayu directs the process of breathing.)

Vayu breathes Hari's name 360 times an hour;
The all-knowing, merciful Lord sends people
To earth, heaven and hell depending on their action. (1)

900 breaths an hour are the work day and night;
Of Vayu who protects all beings;
He lives in the lotus-feet of Moolesha named Hari. (2)

2700 breaths for three hours; for the second half 5400;
For nine hours 8100 and for twelve, 10800 breaths. (3)

Vayu per day utters Mukunda's name 21800 times in breath;
He does this, makes others do it; praise
Vayu for he protects the world. None else can
Do this. (Indra and others), (4)

Merciful Vayu utters Hari's name through breath
324000 times in 15 days; helps
Devotees cross worldly sorrows to reach heaven and release.

(The reader will have certainly noticed the jugglery of figures, many times mind-boggling, in the calculation of breath from half an hour to one hour and then to half a day to day; it leads one to a week, a fortnight, a month and a year. All this figure-jugglery does no credit to Jagannath Dasa's poetic genius. The translator is fully convinced of the surreptitious hand of an interpolator who has turned out poor poetry and heaped it on the great *Harikathamrutasara.*

It is true that Jagannath Dasa was a great devotee of Guru Madhvacharya and that he wants to propagate Madhva Siddanta in his poem. But all that could have certainly be achieved, and is gloriously done, by the acknowledged master-poet. He did have no reason to resort to arithmetic calculations to expound Madhva Siddhanta. All the stanzas in the *magnum opus* are not the great Dasa's because many of them are inferior poetically, aesthetically and semantically. They have been smuggled into *Harikatha* like fakes into devotees' company.)

Two months are a season; there will be 1296000 breaths;
In six months 3888000; thus should the learned
understand. (6)

In a year Guru Madhva does double breath-prayers;
Thus he helps devotees; even in demons he
Makes them to the prayers. (7)

Not realising this people bathe in water,
Sit on a deer skin in style and make a show;
What use is all this? (8)

Food and water merge in water; Rudra and
Vayu patrons of both merge in Rama; Rama
Along with all merges in Madhusudan; thinking
Thus offer food and water to others and have it yourself. (9)

Goats, sheep eat Babul leaves and offer enough milk;
Likewise Laxmi's consorts accepts even the little
That devotees offer; places them in His world,
And grants blessings. Shri Rama supports them. (10)

Of Moon, Sun, fire, black, white and red colour patrons
Shiva, Vayu
Resort to Laxmi who is Krishna, Hayavadana, Janardana.
These on earth protect people in the form of
Food, water and fire. (energy) (11)

Even with lamp not seeing, one may fall into a well;
Likewise people recite meanings of Veda and Upanishad
Not knowing Hari's forms and activities.

They destroy themselves believing being (Jeeva) as
Independent doer and not Hari. (12)

Vayu, worshipped by sages, King of Vedanta
Writers Garuda, Shesha, Rudra, resides in
Agni, Varuna and Indra who are learned;
Vayu prays to Hari and protects us. (13)

Vangmaya, Manomaya are feet; in them
Live Narasimha and Sankarshana; Hari
Makes people study Veda and Shastra to save them. (14)

Like breeze spreading lotus fragrance and
Giving pleasure to nose, enjoy seeing people who
Utter Indiresha's name and act deaf and dumb to others. (15)

To the east of Hari's palace is Sun;
In him are Vayu who again is in Narayana.
People should utter His name and be happy. (16)

To the south of Ompatron (Hari) is Moon with Rohini;
In him are Vyasa named Vayu who again is
Krutipati Pradyumna. Praising Him wander
Fearlessly groups of ancestors. (17)

To the west of brave warrior Hari's Vaikuntha in Agni;
In him are Swahadevi and a host of devotees
In Apana Vayu who praises the Lord; he is in Sankarshana
Whom sages pray and roam around. (18)

To the north of Hari's place are Tumburu;
In them are Vayu containing Gandharvas and
They meditate on blue-coloured Aniruddha. (19)

Garuda, Shesha, Indra, Pushkara and others
Standing on upper part of door join the
Auspicious Lord's house and watching Mukunda
are happy. (20)

Of the five gatekeepers are Bharati's five forms

Vayu's five forms; hidden in them are five
Forms of Laxmi's consort. They evaluate
Entrants' qualities and release them from the world. (21)

Cleanly washed jug shines; after washing body
Applying caste marks if one indulges in
Criticising Madhva's Shastra, he will never
Understand this poem. (22)

Like sea-waves seemingly separate, Hamsa,
Hari, Hayavadana, Krishna and other
Incarnations and His forms in many
Creations appear separate but are all one. (23)

Like water animals moving in water to
Always enjoy, three worlds are in Hari's belly.
They are reflections and Hari's forms. (24)

Like a pregnant woman eating delicious
Things for her child to grow in womb,
Janardana, Ganga's father, defectless,
Eats everything and makes others grow. (25)

Greedy man becomes a slave; one who has
Enslaved greed has others as slaves; one
Who worships Laxmi-consort's feet with devotion
Will make Him give up Laxmi and Himself. (26)

Not knowing the source and the end of Ganga
If one bathes, his sins will get washed;
Likewise he who worships one of myriad qualities
Of Hari, will be surely blessed. (27)

Vasudeva is in cotton, Sankarshana in flax,
Pradymna in thread, Aniruddha in cloth;
Narayana is worshipped and makes others
Worship and is the Centre Ornament. (28)

Jagannath Vitthal with His spouse, like
Cloth is spread warp and weft in the world;
Even in cold, heat, rain and storm He protects
Us; worship Him. (29)

Canto XVI

GIFT OF FREEDOM

(Living being is actively involved in many duties from morning till evening. All these activities are dedicated to God full-heartedly. But this does not mean that God is dependent on man and has to be at man's disposal. Actually God is totally independent. It is man who obtains the so-called freedom from God. Man or living being is dependent and helpless. All of us are in the hands of God.

Jagannath Dasa, in this canto, decribes to what extent God has given freedom to living begins and what the beings do or should do.)

Kind Lord has taken out his 400 freedom qualities
Given 671/4 to Laxmi; 132/4 retained in
His body; thus has Tripada divided. (1)

52 in Bramha, 48 in Yayu, 20 in Rudra,
Kama and Indra 15, Tatvapatrons 10 and
All beings 10; thus Hari has distributed. (2)

45 parts in Kali and other demons; remember
Lord who has partitioned thus; move around as
His servant, He will be your friend. (3)

Like a king who administers passing authority
To ministers, Hari, worshipped by wise, given
All authority to Gods; works and makes them work. (4)

Merciful Lord differentiates sin from merit
Is praised by good; punishes the wicked;
Heeds to devotees' call to grant happiness. (5)

Merchant gets a diamond from a fool
Gives seeds in return to make him happy;
Likewise He accepts demons' sacrifices, grants

Worldly pleasures and makes them bigoted. (6)
Moons's rays remove darkness; Garuda-rider
Likewise grants knowledge and happiness to His
worshippers. (7)

A king will grant pardon to a thief who
Turns in stolen goods; or he will punish him;
Likewise Madhav will accept all our actions
Offered to Him and blesses. (8)

Named Anna (food) Annada (foodgiver) Annada (consumer)
Hari enters living beings, works and makes
Them work; Hari devoid of three qualities
Tests beings for them to be good. (9)

Will a drop of water change an ocean of milk?
Water becomes milk; thus Hari, remover
Of sin, purifies sins and makes them good. (10)

Like a mother lovingly embracing and kissing
Her child and breastfeeding, Lord of unlimited
Qualities presents Himself to a devotee to grant
him pleasure. (11)

Like a gardener to grow crop waters plants
With pot and water carrier, Hayavadana
Creates beings and ever protects them suitably. (12)

A thirsty man not knowing groundwater
Looks at sky and searches for water; likewise
Not realising omnipresent Hari fools worship other gods. (13)

The best reward is obtaining Vaikuntha; Mahar-
loka and Janoloka are middle-level; worldly
Pleasures are inferior; think thus and worship
Hari; Your sorrows will disappear; He protects. (14)

Like a mother giving medicine to her ailing
Child in jaggery-water, Badarayana, the
All-knowing, for devotees' sake has declared

How good deeds will yield merit. thus says He
In Bhagawat and other writings. (15)

Distance lends enchantment; when near is found full
Of snakes and wild animals; worldly
Pleasures, likewise, are unworthy; wise therefore
Worship Rama's consort. (16)

Mud vessels though dried in summer-sun
Cannot hold liquid; likewise food saying,
"I am independent" and fasting, offering
Charity creates only his physical worry. (17)

Learn from the wise external discipline
And internal discipline; give up hatred;
Remember Hari, the Supreme, worshipped by
Rama, Bramha and others. (18)

To Hari there's nothing low or pleasure-giving;
No justice or injustice; no hatred or jealousy;
Has no parents; Him remembered even laughingly, He will
Make us float in the worldly ocean. (19)

Let him be ignorant; after bath if he wears
Caste-marks, basil and lotus-seed garlands,
And prays to Mukund, Lord of earth, him
Hari will protect. (20)

You appear to be leader, lord, because of your
Youth and wealth; were you a lord when you
Were in mother's womb? When dead lordship,
Wealth will disappear. (21)

Vasudeva alone is Lord; Bramha, Rudra, Indra
Are His servants; giving up the royal road
If one thinks himself to be god, why is he
Not saved from bodily and other sorrows? (22)

Lord in the three worlds in omnipresent, organiser,
Creator, controller and director; the six qualities

Leave Him not like service leaving not living beings. (23)
Ever new, unaffected, friend like life, originator of Om,
Language, mind, Sama-favourite, Dattatraya,
Kapil, Hayavadana-formed Lord resides in
All beings and works according to their merit. (24)

Shrutis are His speech; Smrutis His orders;
Life and Prakuti are His forms; offering all
Actions to Hari ask not worldly pleasures. (25)

Like a king giving salary to his servants
According to their service, Vasudeva, grants
Good qualities to devotees and makes them happy. (26)

Lamp is extinguished in day; the same near
God is Nandadeepa; this is no ritual;
Work of good people though bad is merit;
Work of the wicked attracts punishment. (27)

Go to teach Shastra to people like a salesman
Who moves from house to house; read to and teach
The good; even in dream shun the bad; Shri Hari will bless
you. (28)

To the living work, duty and wealth always are fascinating;
Remove the fascinations; remember all-free, world-supporter,
Hari. (29)

If sense organs were to work why does a sleeping
Man no answer give? God gives him waking stage
He then does work. If like were free why does
Man not control waking stage, dream, total
Sleep and unconsciousness? (30)

This is no idle talk; these are words of Shruti Smruti;
These are stepping-stones to release; devotional
Worship will earn Hari's grace and happiness. (31)

Word and mind patrons are Parvati Parameshwara;
Their Lord Shrinivasa is offered all qualities

Like beads threaded in the string of knowledge.
The ignorant consider this foolish like a monkey not know
diamond value; (32)

Narayana, with His Lotus-feet worshipped by
Laxmi, Bramha, Vayu, Garuda, Shesha, Rudra, Indra,
Manmath, Sun, Moon, Sages of the world, Gandharva,
Kinnara, Siddha, Sadhya, grants protection to His
devotees. (33)

Learned and the ignorant may call a mirror ("Kannadi" in
Kannada) Adarsha
In Sanskrit or use the local language-word,
Still will they not see their face in it? Likewise a book
About Hari's exploits may be in Kannada, will
Not the wise enjoy it? (34)

Not praising the sun a thief may hate him;
Will this touch the Sun? The wicked may
Hate this book because it is not in Sanskrit;
Will not Hari bless people who devotionally
listen to this? (35)

Can a leather-bag containing Ganga-water
Be holy? Likewise Sanskrit poems by others
Are unworthy; Hari's story though in Prakrit (Kannada)
Is fit to lead one to salvation. (36)

I have read no Veda, Shastra, Logic, Meemansa;
Not have I heard them; company of the good
Has not come to me always; I have, with the kindness
Of Madhva followers, told what Jagannath Vitthal
Has told me. (37)

(Jagannath Dasa has repeated why *Harikatha* written in Kannada, not in Sanskrit, be read with care, love and devotion. Sanskrit was the language of scholarship and worship. Any religious activity to be acceptable was to be in Sanskrit. Jagannath Dasa, curiously enough, defends his poem written in Kannada. Before his initiation as Dasa he used to contemptuously look at Kannada poems written by the Dasa. Now he comes to his own defence several times. His final consolation or victory is that the entire poem has been formed, created and retold to him by Jagannath Vitthal.)

Canto XVII

DISTRIBUTION OF FREEDOM

(This canto is named "Svagata Swatantrya Sandhi" or "Swatantraya Vibhaga Sandhi" by some publishers. The Lord has partitioned a part of His unlimited independence and distributed that part among other lower gods. Bramha and others share the small freedom.)

Hari took out a portion of His freedom
And distributed it among Bramha and others;
Bhrugu sage told this to King Indradumna.
Vishnu is supreme, totally free; Maya, ever-young,
Laxmi resides in Hari's heart; Bramha Vayu
Being ministers are Hari's favourites; ego-patrons,
Rudra, Indra and Sun are sense organ-masters. (1)

Kali and demons reside in living beings and promote sins;
Like Bramha Kali too is ego-patron; wretched Madhu,
Mean Kaitabha,[1] angry Shankhara are mind-patrons. (2)

(Note [1] : Madhu and Kaitabha are names of dangerous demons.)

Like gods these reside in different organs and are active;
Hari, has apportioned freedom like servant-salary-
distribution. (3)

Making four parts of unlimited freedom
One part is selected for ten parts; 4/5 of this
Is in Vayu, all five quarters in Bramha;
The second part has ten and two are in Rudra. (4)

One and a half in Indra and Kama, one in
Ten organ patrons, one in all beings, Kali and
Other demons have four and a half. The remaining
Two parts are divided into three and giving
One to Laxmi, Hari has retained the balance. (5)

Rama's consort has thus distributed freedom
Among gods, humans and demons and enjoys.
Makes them do duty, watches impartially
Grants them at age-end (Yuganta) rewards suitably. (6)

Like a lamp shining according to its size;
Hari exists everywhere. With Shri, Earth and
Durga He plays in the world to grant beings blessings. (7)

Actions, good and bad, done by organs,
If offered to Lord will be accepted; He accepts
Good deeds, destroys bad; with haters of
His devotees He accepts their merit and
Transfers bad deeds of His Devotees. (8)

One who hates not doers of bad deeds,
Who praises not seniors' deeds and qualities,
Obtains sin of cow, Brahmin and woman murder.
This is according to Shastra. (9)

Giving His freedom-qualities to Bramha
Kali and others, Hari makes them do
Duties related to their merit and sin.
Even low beings are protected and blessed. (10)

Is there a country where day and night come together?
Cold and heat don't bother mountains. Likewise
As a lotus-leaf Hari existing in many lives
Makes them do duties. (11)

He divides merit and sin among Brahma
And others; lives in beings who are His
Reflections; all this, like big and small
Pots filling water to suit their size. (13)

One should with no contempt listen to
Vishnu's enchanting story told by Bhrugu
To king Indradumna; the learned need
Ignore unpalatable words in it. (14)

Devotees, who believe in Jagannath Vitthal,
Fearless, Lord of world, Bramha's father,
Kansa-killer, Madhva's friend, Protector of
All, Myriad sun-bright, Supreme, Saviour
Of Ahalya, saver of orphans, and chief
Guru, will certainly receive protection. (15)

Canto XVIII

PLAYFUL LORD

(Lord lives in everyone independently and makes them perform their work. He is supreme and above Bramha and other gods. He makes them work as His servants or instruments. Jagannath Dasa narrates how Hari performs duties through other gods and living beings.)

When supplicated respectfully for Srinivasa's story,
Soota took pity on Shaunaka and others;
He told the story.
Can beings perform actions such as eating,
Digesting, moving, swallowing, talking,
Sex, sleep, seeing, walking, not walking?
Hari in every being makes them do actions
Suited to them. (1)

Entering body He works in many ways
And is called "living". His dependents feel happy
When the Lord leaves the body people call it corpse and hate it. (2)

For play He gives different bodies; exists in Bramha
Rudra and others and demons and performs many
Activities; He gets no reward. (3)

Hari is President of Bramha, Vayu, Rudra, Indra,
Acts with no return; indestructible, realformed,
Strange (incomprehensible) Hari protects the world. (4)

Laxmi, Saraswati, Bharati, Parvati, Shachi, Rati,
Rohini, Sanjna, Shatarupa are women in female form.
He grants them their wishes after they trust Him. (5)

Like children playing with stick-horse, Hari
Granting freedom to Bramha and Others, sports;

Non-visible self is favourable to devotees but
unfavourable to demons. (6)

Hari, Garuda-rider, protector, Supreme being,
All-knowledge store, is called by many names,
Has many forms; living in them He makes them work to suit
their merit or sin. (7)

Who, except those abandoning all daily pleasures
Meditate on God, can understand Hari's greatness?
Can those indulging in pleasures of food, sleep and sex know
Him? (8)

How can dullards understand Hari's blessings of release?
Not knowing momentary pleasures, mountain of sorrows
And worshipping other gods, how can they earn release? (9)

Like a king granting administration to ministers,
And rewarding and punishing, Janardana
Unconquerable, resides in all and makes them work. (10)

To grant freedom to Bramha and other gods
And demons Hari divides in half; making four
Quarters each one with 100 parts, He gives 52 to Bramha,
48 to Vayu and half to Saraswati and Bharati. (11)

The second quarter is made into 100 parts; 20 to Rudra,
15 to Indra, 15 to Kama, 10 to all other gods;
All living beings have 10 and demons 45. (12)

The merciful Lord has made three parts of the balance half,
Given one to Laxmi, taken two for self.
Like a king after allotting authority to servants
Asks for an account, He expresses Himself in beings' actions.
(13)

Merit-doing devotees obtain merit even of Kali;
Sin committed by gods is transferred to the wicked;
thus does Hari administer His creation. (14)

One who says that Hari has His equal is contemptuous;
It is he who misrepresents Hari's teaching; hates
Wearers of caste marks; indulges in non-godly
Talk; these are demons. They hate the work of the wise;
Worshipping low things waste life in ignorance;
They are full of lust, avarice, anger, violence,
Falsehood, hypocrisy and cunning; they differentiate
Hari's forms; call Him sorrowful; eat flesh and
Drink prohibited things; are in wicked company;
Are despicable and condemnable. (15,16,17)

The good have knowledge, devotion, renunciation,
Humility, listening to Purana and learning, charity
Control, performing sacrifice, truth, non-violence, mercy
Meditation, Lord's story-telling, silence, rituals,
Counting beads, penance, bath in holy waters, Mantra,
Prayers, prostration. (18)

With very little freedom given to beings they
Show merit and sin. Beings indulge in
Breathing, eating, drinking, sleeping, romantic
Sex, moving, suffering joys and sorrows,
Dreaming, sleep-awakening. (19)

As told before half freedom is with Hari;
The other half is distributed among Bramha,
Vayu, Shiva, who enjoy happiness. (20)

(The reader can easily recollect how Jagannath Dasa has repeated the same thought. He has said that Hari has distributed freedom in a particular way. In two or three cantos he repeats it and creates boredom. The beauty of the poem suffers a great deal by such uninteresting repetitions. The translator has also to restate that all these torturous repetitions must have been the creation of an inferior writer who has tagged on his indifferent work to the great Dasa's *Harikatha*.)

Not realising that Hari in us is doing everything
And arrogating His work to self, people obtain
Demons' sins and lose their merits. He grants
Them to other devotees. (21)

The sun moves, shades of trees change;

Likewise since Hari exists everywhere the wise
Know merit and sin. They sing of Laxmipati's
greatness. (22)

Laxmi, original Prakruti, resides everywhere
And sports; when she offers her Lord merit and sin
Of beings, sins turn to merit like water
Changed to milk when mixed with milk-ocean. (23)

What can duties do to wisdom-incarnate Lord?
Can insects eat fire? One who can destroy
Everything is not touched by sins. (24)

To joyful Hari what is dear is head; right
Side is joy; left is special joy; thus speak
Shrutis. Moda (dear) is worldly pleasure,
Pramoda is other worldly pleasure; Since Hari
Grants both, He is called Moda and Pramoda. (25)

After rain will all water joining sea
Make the sea overfull? With no rain will it dry?
Thus defectless Hari is least affected by
Merit and sin of living beings. (26)

Life (Jiva) and Paramatma are the two birds living closely
In body-tree; life enjoys result of its actions;
Paramatma offers sins to His haters, demons. (27)

Like darkness disappearing with Sun, Hari's
Presence drives away all sins. Like fire Hari
Burns sins even of Bramha and other gods. (28)

A bit of 10 parts of 400 is granted to insects;
He grants joy to gods and demons suited
To their actions; mindless animals, ants,
Insects are given food, joy, death and suffering. (29)

Kali, with his gang, reaches unreturnable
Dark well-like world; Bramha and others
Praise the Lord and obtain release. (30)

Offer all actions to Madhusudana; He grants
Merit to gods, sin to demons; if not offered
Demons, like thieves stealing fruits of unprotected garden,
Steal your merit. (31)

A lamp drinking only oil leaving dirt, He
Grants merit acquired by Kali and demons
To Bramha and other gods. (32)

Fire though burning everything is considered
To be pure by Shruti and Smruti; gods doing
Demerits intentionally offer them to Him;
He accepts them and protects. (33)

Will anyone pluck fruits of a guarded garden?
None would even dare to see them. Our actions,
Our family, children, wife are His servants;
Thought thus we burn our sins. (34)

Offer all actions done by mental and
Physical organs; Hari accepting them will
Relieve you of birth-rebirth; if unoffered
All merits will be snatched by demons. (35)

Proud people, learned in Shruti Smruti,
May acquire merit; Hari accepts it not;
Grants them sins of the good; His
Supremacy accepted will drive away mental and
Physical sufferings. (36)

Think that Bramha and others are servants,
Rama's consort alone is free; offer merit and
Sins to Him; He will transfer sins to demons to
punish them. (37)

Existing in cruel demons Hari is called Kubera;
He can enter everyone, so is called Niruta;
Understood by the wise and called Surya;
Remover of suffering, so is Shukla; has
No body, so is Akaya. (38)

To destroy incalculable sins utter Hari;
Kind Lord will lead even such people to His abode
For eternal happiness. (39)

Like a patient getting well by medicine and
Diet, listen to Bhagawat, conquer worldly ills,
Offer all actions to Hari in whom is Vayu;
Guru Jagannath Vitthal will be pleased. (40)

Canto XIX

RELEASE FROM ACTION

(This canto is called "Shri Hari Stotra" by some publishers. Beings may follow all principles enunciated by the Shastras. They may perform rituals very meticulously. Still they may commit sins. One day's sin may lead to ten births in the lowest from. So, a wise man should do his duties according to his conscience. He should study Madhva philosophy, pray to God and seek good people's company. Offering his actions to Hari is the only course open to him.)

Narayana is the prime cause; he creates Avatars;
Snake-formed Jayapati Sankarshana exists everywhere;
Pradyumna lives inside-outside in all lives. (1)

Five are world's causes; each one has five with
25 forms; Hari enjoys in the world in 30 forms;
Merciful Lord, all intelligent, supports the world that is inside
belly. (2)

Action, cause and doer, all-in-one Kapil-named
Hari sports with His family. He is motivator,
Not motivated; being senior to Rama, Bramha
He protects the world with His strength. (3)

Lord in the world assumes Vyaptaruma in sky,
Aveshrupa, Avatararupa and Antaratmaka; being
Indestructible, living in Yogis' heart, Hari supports all. (4)

Like different fire in wood and stone merciful Lord,
Being cause and action lives in all incognito and grants
blessings suitably. (5)

Like sea-waves the oncoming merit-sin consequences
Are given to beings; He makes them do them and
Creates suffering; He accepts not wicked peoples'

Worship; He is not proud; is healthy, independent,
Philosopher, intelligent, unrivalled, Laxmi's consort. (6)

Clouds and submarine fire drink sea-water;
Clouds bring rain and grant peace; fire swallows;
Likewise Hari swallows peoples' merit and sin. (7)

Not realising that Hari is no-reward-aspirant,
Makes people work, one can read books, tell beads
From morning to evening; what use is it all? (8)

Will a wine pot be purified by dipping it every day in Ganga water?
Not praising Hari purposefully will lead one wrong.
It may give more sorrow. (9)

Worship the Supreme Hari by devotionally praising Him;
Follow actions stipulated by Smruti and Shruti
As orders of Hari, abandon worldly pleasures and useless talk. (10)

Non-expected action offered to Hari, will be
Purified of sins; He will ignore sins and grant blessings. (11)

If one praises Hari to protect, He will grant release;
Hari is Himself, joy incarnate, devotee-approachable,
Supporter of world, sorrowless, with lotus-feet,
Worshipped by gods, and Madhva followers,
Most charming, a patron of followers, eternally
Merciful and Lotus-eyed. (12)

Purifying self, offer all actions to Hari named Sudharma,
Bramha's father will show mercy and place
Him in His palace and support. (13)

Patron of the followers, Hari always grants blessings
To devotees; worship Him, Shesha-sleeper, not
For petty wordly pleasures; Like a sculptor making
An idol from any stone, Krishna lifts the low. (14)

Sky, with a place-change, may appear different;
Likewise existing in all Hari may appear different;
Living in our bodily actions like hatred,
Love and dejection, He grants rewards suitably. (15)

Worship Bramha's father, your past and future actions are destroyed;
He shines like lightening in our heart-sky; Lord
Favours not the deceitful; He wears Koustubha
Diamond, and is auspicious and praised by gods. (16)

The simple living beings can never overcome sins
Despite good deeds; not concentrating on Him
Fixed like a flow of oil, fools believe in actions as saviours. (17)

Bramha, Indra and other gods, not fully
Comprehending His greatness by mind, words, resort
To Hari like a shade to a tree; devotionally they
Praise Him with "Oh Laxmi's Consort, protect us." (18)

Frog is a water animal; how can man cross
An ocean riding a frog? Likewise ignorant
People worship Sun, Shiva ignoring the Supreme
Hari. How can they prosper? (19)

A hungry man trying to eat berries
And falling into a thorny bush; unlike him one should
Meditate on Hari and not fall a prey to
Fake sadhus who work to fill their belly. (20)

Being a king's son and asking for a coin, or asking for dung of a wish fulfilling cow, don't
Forget Krishna; ask not worldly pleasures
But fall at His feet and pray. (21)

Like giving up fast on Shivaratri, Dwadashi, Dashami,
Ancestor Shraddha, Shravana Nakshtra, give up illegal
Wealth; meditate on in Anandatirtha (Madhva). (22)

Like fasting on Amavasya coming in morning,
Full Monday in Adhika month, Shravan coming
After 12 hours, Ekadashi, offer all action to Hari;
He will grant release. (23)

Existing in mind as knowledge, knowable,
Knower; Hari called knowledge-patron shining as moon in sages
Shuka Shounaka, will be yours. (24)

Lord will, like He did to Sudama, be pleased with
Those who praise lovingly His greatness; He is
Laxmi's consort, master of Vayu, Lord of three worlds,
Mass of good qualities, master of all gods. (25)

Like a child separated from his parents
But in distant country identifying parents
Of boys like him and saying, "May be my parents
Like them," wise try to find out in Shruti Purana
Lord Krishna's form and delve deep in the
Ocean of literature. (26, 27)

Shout, "Manmatha's father, saviour of devotees,
Laxmi's consort, Vaikuntha master, protect me";
Like calf running at mother-cow's voice He
Will eagerly run to His devotees. (28)

Near the wise; away from the wicked;
Unavailable to demon group; like Garuda fond
Of worldly serpent, Hari comes to protect devotees. (29)

He created Ganga; wears conch, disc, male;
Invincible; unavailable to fools; lotus-feet
Worshipped by Bramha, Rudra and others;
Born as Trivikrama to destroy Bali's sacrifice. (30)

None to equal Hari among gods; supreme
All the time, to all people; give up worldly
Thoughts when listening to such Hari's story. (31)

Bestower of wishes to the worshippers; precious
Diamond to devotees; wearer of jewellery;
Merciful; Unaffected by three qualities;
Incomprehensible Lord ignores devotees'faults.
Did not Rama accept Shabari's fruits? (32)

None to say "He knows Him fully"; none to
Reject Him; no place where He is absent;
He is everywhere like jaggery-toy; Shridevi,
Bhudevi's Consort has no equal to Him. (33)

Understood by Vedas, remover of devotees' miseries,
Upendra, Yadu leader, incomparable, extraordinary
In good qualities, such Hari readily favours
His devotees. Like fire in wood He exists in them. (34)

Jagannath Vitthal, saluted by Rama and
Bramha, was, like common people, born to Devaki.
Brother of Balarama He protects those who
Depend on Him and punishes demons. (35)

Canto XX

ON DIFFERENTIATION

(One of the tenets of Madhva Siddhanta is the Taratamya Bhava or differentiation that exists among god's creation. The great sage Vyasa was once asked to enunciate the basic principles of Madhva philosophy to which he immediately replied :

"Shriman Madhvamate Harih Paratarao
Satyam Jagattatwatah Bhedo Jivaganah" etc.

In the reply the expression "Bhedo Jivaganah" points out that there is Taratamya Bhava among God's creation.

Jagannath Dasa, an ardent disciple of Madhva philosophy and its propagators has devoted a few cantos to explain the differentiation. Except Shri Hari who is Supreme, infallible, omnipresent, omniscient, omnipotent, eternal, the One and the only one, all other creations of God are controlled by Him who sports with His creations. Each god, rushi, wise sages and men are of different levels. Jagannath Dasa has explained the theory of differentiation in the *Harikatha.*)

Let Jagannath, the merciful, always pure,
Veda-knower, conqueror of birth life and death,
Omnipresent, served by the released and the unreleased,
Truth-incarnate, eternal, remover of fear, favourite of devotees,
Protect me.
He is worshipped by Shri, Bhu, Durgapati, Bramha
Existing in and out of world, who is served
With Shesha's hood as umbrella, who is away
From sins and prohibited activities. (1 and 2)

Rama sees Hari's qualities and forms anew
Everytime like water in flowing Ganga. She is
Incomparable, defectless, joyful, ornament
To Hari; destroys His enemies. (3)

Eternally released, emotion and other quality-free,
Mother to sinless Bramha-Vayu, always young,

Laxmi is lower by numberless qualities than Hari.
Thus speak Vedas and Puranas. (4)

Bramha and Vayu are equal; worship Hari
The same way, are served by Rudra and other gods,
And called Apa Bramha; Rama is superior to
These by a crore Sajati [1] qualities; Bramha Vayu
Are inferior to her by a crore Vijati qualities. (5)

(Note [1] : Sajati qualities are of the same nature; Vijati qualities are qualities different. An example is given by Shri Sankarshana Wodeyar in his commentary. Vedas are four; One has read two of them; another has read four. Two Vedas read by both are Sajati. Two others are Vijati; a person who has read four Vedas is superior to the one who has read only two. Likewise Bramha-Vayu and Laxmi have some common qualities; They are shared qualities. There and in unshared qualities Laxmi is superior to Bramha-Vayu.)

Saraswati, Bharati have 100 Vijati qualities than their husband; Saraswati, the wise say, is superior slightly to Bharati. (6)

Garuda, Shesha, Rudra are equal. These three are
Inferior to Saraswati by 100 qualities; Rudra
By position is slightly inferior to Shesha; Krishna's
Six queens are inferior to Rudra by five qualities;
They are superior to Varuni, Sauparni and Parvati by two qualities. (7)

Garuda-Shesha-Rudras' wives Sauparni, Varuni,
Parvati are less by 10 qualities; Parvati is
Inferior to Varuni; Indra, Kama are inferior to
Parvati by ten qualities; Kama is positionally
Inferior to Indra. (8)

Ahankarika Prana is by 10 qualities inferior to Indra-Kama;
Aniruddha, Rati, Swayambhuva Manu, Daksha,
Bruhaspati, Shachi are equal; Pravahavayu
is inferior to them by 5 qualities. (9)

Vivaswan named Sun, Moon, Yama, Svayambhu-
Manu's wife, Shatarupa, are two qualities less than
Pravahavayu;
Varuna is 3/8 quality less than Sun; Narada is

1/8 quality less than Varuna; less by 1/8 quality
Are Bhrugu, Agni, Prasutis. (10)

Bramha's sons Marichi, Atri, Angiras, Pulastya,
Krutu, Vashishta, Vaivaswata Mani, Vishwamitra,
All seven are 2 qualities less than Agni; Mitra
A little less than Vishwamitra; Kubera and
Vishwaksena are less than Tara. (11)

(Barring the 15 gods already mentioned) 85 gods
Are equal to Kubera, Vishwaksena and Ganesha. They
Are 6 Suns, 47 Marudganas, 7 Vasus, 10 Rudras, 10
Vishwadevate, 2 Ashwinis, Rubbu, Pitru and Earth. (12)

Chavana, Sanakasa, Pavaka, Shukra, Uchithya,
Jayant, Kashyapa, Ekadasha Manu, Dhruva,
Nahusha, Shatabindu, Kartiviryarijuna,
Dushyanta, Bali and 7 Indras, Kakushtha
And Gaya are lower than 85 gods. (13)

Pruthu, Shakuntala, Bharata, Mandhata
Priyavruta, Maruta, Pralhad, Parikshit,
Harishchandra, Ambarisha, Uttanapada, all 100 pious
People are called action-patron gods with a bit of
Hari's divinity.
Priyavrata is superior by 2 qualities to all these. (14)

Ganga, Sanjna, Rohini, Shyamalà, Usha and
Parjanya are 2 qualities less than action-patrons.
Swaha is 2 less than Ganga, Usha and Shani
2 qualities less. (15)

Action-lord Pushkara is less than Usha by 2;
Ajanaja gods are better than Chirapitru; but
Are servants of Pushkara and 10 less; Ajanaja
Are singers in Indra's court and equal to them
Are a hundred less than 9 crore Rushis. (16)

Wives of Gandharva and Rushis are equal;
Human Gandharva are less by 12 qualities than

Divine Gandharva; earthly emperors and their
Wives are less by 10; best men are 100 less
Good entirely, good moderately, good and bad;
Bad and good devotees are fit for salvation;
Moderately moderate are of the world; born
On earth they enjoy in heaven; moderate and bad are born on earth but go to hell. (18)

Demons are bad and good; are large in number,
Famous and as a group are bad and moderate; Kali's wife
Jeshtha is bad; Kali, a mine of bad qualities,
Despicable and worst of the worst. (19)

There's none wicked like him in three worlds;
A home of hatred; is spread among butchers,
Gold, prostitutes, gambling, liquor, falsehood;
Infatuates people and ruins. These be avoided. (20)

Merciful Hari, sleeper on Shesha, has created
Three types of beings; sports with His wives; people
Who know god-demon differentiation are relieved from the world. (21)

Difference is soul for Madhva Siddanta;
Like fire to a forest of sin, a new boat
To cross worldly ocean and a step towards release. (22)

Knowledge of differentiation is a gate to salvation;
The wise should learn from the seniors, teach the
Devotees and make them happy. "Mithya philosophers"
(Advaitins) find it harsh; teach not the wicked;
Teach the good only. (23)

I salute Shri Hari, Laxmi, Bramha, Vayu, Saraswati-
Bharati, Garuda-Shesha-Rudra, Krishna's 6 queens,
Parvati-Sauparni-Varuni, Indra-Manmath,
Prana, Aniruddha, Shachi, Guru, Rati,
Swayambhuva Manu, Daksha-Pravaha, Maruta,
Manavi, Shatarupa, Yama-Chandra-Surya,
Varuna-Narada, Agni-Prasuti, Bhrugu sages,

Bramha's children, great penance-makers Atri,
Marichi, Vaivaswata Manu, Acharya Patni-Tara,
Mitra, Niruti, Pravaha Patni-Pravahi, Kubera,
Shiwini gods, Ganapati, Vishwakesena, other
100 gods, Manus, Rushis. (24 and 25)

100 merit-holder Kings, Bhagirathi,
Virat, Parjanya, Rohini, Shyamala, Sanjna,
Swaha, Buddha, Usha, Shani, Pushkar, all I salute. (26)
Shrikrishna's 1600 wives, Agastya and
Other great sages, Urvasi and other heavenly damsels,
100 Tumburu kindly make me sing Krishna's songs. (27)

Ajanaja gods who not given Soma juice and
Not very popular, human singers, heavenly
Singers, King, earthly Vaishnavas and
Best among men I salute everyday happily. (28)

(The readers will again notice the many repetitious stanzas in the canto. The only explanation is that Jagannath Dasa wants to emphasize again and again Madhva philosophical tenets, repeats them to carry their effect on the readers. However, *Harikatha's* poetic qualities suffer a great deal because of repetitious string of names of gods and sages.)

The devotees who understand differentiation
In the best of men to
Bramha by 100 qualities Jagannath Vitthal will bless;
The differentiation be respectfully followed. (29)

Canto XXI

BROAD DIFFERENTIATION

(The present canto is called "Anshavacharana Sandhi" or "Aveshavatara Sandhi". In this Shri Hari's and other gods' Avataras, divine qualities and other vital matters have been discussed.)

Always meditate on Hari, Laxmi, Bramha, Vayu
And their power, (entering into) incarnations and qualities.

Fish, Tortoise, Hog, Man-lion, Vamana, Parashurama, Rama
Buddha, Kalki Kapil, Vaikuntha, Srinivasa,
Vyasa, Bull, Hayagriva, Mohini, Swan,
Aniruddha, Trivikrama, Shridhara, Ajit,
Harushikesha and others are Lord's Avataras. (1)

Hari is Narayana; demon-destroyer Krishna
Is bright as sun; defectless, complete and
Supreme Lord, Omnipresent, Best of men,
Ancient, deathless, is Vasudeva and has other incarnations. (2)

Bramha's mother, Laxmi, by Hari's grace
Is full of knowledge, strength and devotion;
She less than Hari in many qualities
Has no equal among other gods. (3)

Shri, Bhu, Durga, Ambhrisha, Satyabhama,
Shanti, Kruti, Jaya, Maya, Mahalaxmi,
Sita, Dakshina, are goddesses of three worlds;
They are atom-size and huge and incomparable. (4)

Bramha Vayu are 1 crore qualities less than Laxmi
By the grace of the Lord, not bothering much
About Garuda, Shesha, Rudra, they live in all beings. (5)

Bramha's names are Virinchi, Purusha, Maha;

Marut, Mukhya Prana, Dhruti, Smruti, Guru-
Vara Mahadhyata, Balwant, Vijnana,
Vikhyata, Garalabhuk, Bhavarogbheshaja,
Virabhaya and Bhima are Vayu's names. (6)

Vayu is strong, totally renounced; named
Rochana; grantor of release; is Ananadatirtha;
Chief of gods, conqueror of sleep, beautiful-formed,
Taker of atom-huge forms, incarnation of
Amruta, Hanuma, Bhima, Madhva; future Bramha
He indeed is the path to Hari-understanding. (7)

Vayu Bramha being inferior are servants of
Laxmi; with the form of devotion, knowledge,
Strength they exist in all and grant them fame. (8)

Saraswati is Veda-patron; being Bhuja (one who eats) attends to
Her husband and Narasimha; she is Bramhi,
Grants happiness, is called Shraddha, Priti,
Gayatri and Savitri; mother of Garuda-Shesha;
Was born of Jaya-Sankarshana and is Vani;
She promotes action and sense organs and is revered in 14 worlds. (9)

Kashi King's daughter Kali, Draupadi, Shiva's daughter,
Indrasena, Katabhimani, Chandra, the wise
Bharati and Saraswati are 100 qualities
Less than their husbands. (10)

Hari Vayu joined (inside, incorporated) Avatar is Nara; Sankarshana
Joined is Laxmana; great Shuklakesha joined
Is Balarama; these are Shesha's incarnations;
Rudra's Avataras are Hara, Sadashiva, Tapas,
Ahamkrutu, Shukracharya, Urdhvapata,
Tatpurusha, Jaigeesh, Aurva, Ashwatthama,
Kirat and Durvasa. (11)

Garuda, Shesha, Rudra are equal; lower by

100 qualities than Bharati-Saraswati; Krishna's
Wife Jambuvati has Laxmi joined and is a
Little less than Shesha; other 5 queens are less
By 5 qualities than Garuda-Shesha-Rudra. (12)

Varuni, Sauparni and Parvati are inferior to
Neela, Bhadra, Mitra Vinda, great Kalindi,
Laxmana and Jambuvati; Varuni, being
Balarama's wife named Revati, is a part
Of Shridevi; Parvati and others are 10
Qualities less than their husbands. (13)

Nara-Hari's part is Indra's son Arjuna, and
Gadhiking; Kusha, Mandradyumna, Vikshaki,
Wali and Indra's incarnations; Rama's brother
Bharata, Jambuvati's son Samba, Bramha's
Bit of divinity is Manmatha, Sudarshana,
Pradyumna, Sanaka, Shanmukha, Kama
Are Manmath's Avataras. (14)

Indra-Kama are 10 qualities less than
Parvati-Varuni; Ahankarika Prana is
Is less than Indra by 10 qualities; Aniruddha,
Rati, Daksha, Brahaspati, Shachi, Swayam-
Bhu Mana, - these six are equal and are
Less by 10 qualities than Ahankarika Prana. (15)

Kama's son Aniruddha became Shatrughana; in
Aniruddha Krishna's grandson is Aniruddha named Hari;
Kama's
Wife Rati is Rugmavati, Lakshana (Duryodhana's daughter)
Of good name, Pauluma, Chitrangada, and
Tara (Wali's wife); in these two names are of Shachi. (16)

In Bharata Tatparya Nirnaya (Madhvacharya's work) it is said
that
Brahaspati had three incarnations; in Traita Yuga
A monkey Tara who praised Rama, he was
Krishna's favourite as Uddama; then Drona of Bramha
quality. (17)

Pravaha Vayu is 5 qualities less than Swayambhu Manu;
Surya, Chandra, Yama, Shatarupa are 2
Qualities less than Pravaha; the wise should always
Meditate on Surya (sun), Chandra (moon) and Yama. (18)

Yama, joined by Vayu, has four incarnations;
Dharma, Jambuvanta, Vidura and Satyajit;
Surya, joined by Bramha, is Sugriva, and
Joined by Hari, is Karna; Chandra with
Indra became Angada. (19)

Varuna, 3/8 qualities less than Surya, has
Four incarnations; Mahabhishakraja, Dharma
Raksha Sushena, emperor Shantanu; heavenly
Sage Narada is a little less than Varuna;
Agni, Bhrugu, Daksha's wife Prasuti and inferior to Narada.
(20)

Neela, Dhrushtadyumna, Leva are Agni's incarnations;
Because Bhrugu kicked Hari he was born as
Hunter Jara; all these are lower than Narada
But higher than 7 sages; Pralhad, with Vayu
Element, was their equal and was born Balhika. (21)

Pralhad, one of action-gods, with Narada's grace,
Became equal of Agni, Bhrugu and Daksha's wife
Vaivaswata Manu and Vishwamitra are a little
Inferior to Agni but equal to 7 sages. (22)

Bramha's sons, with controlled senses, are Marichi,
Atri, Angiras, wise Pulaha, Krutu, Vashishta, Pulastya;
These are inferior to Agni a little; Mitra named,
Surya with Rahu element became Bhishmaka;
In Traita Yuga he was born Taraka, A monkey. (23)

Niruti had two incarnations, monkey Durmukh,
Rudra-Element Ghatotkaja; they are equal to
Pravaha's wife Pravahi and Guru's wife Tara.
But they are better than Parjanya; Kubera had
Two incarnations, Rudra's element Bhagadatta

And Katthana monkey; Ganapati was Krishna's
Son Charudeshna; Ganapati and Kubera are
Equal to Ashiwins. (24)

Of Drona, Dhruva, Dosha, Arka, Agni, Prana,
Dyu, Vibhavasu, Ashtavasu, Agni is superior;
With Bramha-element Dyu was born Bhishma;
Vasu Drona was Nandagopa; except main Agni,
Seven Vasus are equal in intelligence. (25)

Eleven Rudras are Bhima, Raivata, Aja, Ajaikapat,
Mohan Bahurupaka, Bhava, Vama, Ugra, Vrusha Kapi,
Ahirbuddhi; among them Bhava named Parvati's
Husband is senior, others are mutually equal. (26)

Ajaikapat was born Bhuri King; with 11 Rudra-element
Ahirbuddhi became Bhrushrava; Virupakshya (Bhava)
Was Shalya; Vishkambaka Rudra became the wise Krupa;
Jarasandha's sons Sahadeva and brave Somadatta
Became Pratapaka's incarnations. (27)

Chief of gods, Indra (Shakra), Urukrama, Mitra,
Varuna, Parjanya, Bhaga, Pusha, Vivaswan, Savita,
Dhata, Aryama, Trushtru are 12 Adityas; Of these
Savitra-named Surya was born as Bhanu to Krishna and
Satyabhama;
Trushtru, with Yama-element, became King Virasena.(28)
Of the 12 Suryas 6 are good, Vivaswan, Varuna,
Shakra, Uru, Krama, Mitra; Paravaha, the great,
With Vayu-element became Pandu; Kesari,
Supati and Sheta were born with Marut-element. (29)

Pratibha named Marut became Chakitanana yadava;
Saumya Marut was Vipruthu Yadava; Prana-named
Marut-element were Vitata and Sarpottunga Yadavas
Became monkey Gaja; another Maruta named Apana
Was Gavaksha; third Vyasa, Udana were monkeys
Vrukshaparva and Vrushabha; great warrior
Bhima's son Sarvatrata and monkey Gandhamada
Are of the same Marut quality. (30)

Of the 5 Nagas Kurma became Kuntibhoja;
Other Nagas, Krukhala, Devadatta and Dhananjaya
Had no incarnations; Kevaha, Udwaha,
Vivaha, Samvaha - all Maruts are a little
Inferior to Marut Pravaha. (31)

Except five, Prana, Apana, Vyana, Udana, Samana
All other Maruts are equal; the 10 Vishwedevas are
Slightly less; they were born as five sons
To revered Draupadi; others are born as
Kaikeyas all the time. (32)

Draupadi's sons Prati Vindhya, Shrutasoma,
Shrutikirti, Shatanika, Shrutakarma, have in them
Gandharva king, Chitraratha's, Gopa, Kishore
And Bala Gandharvas' element; each son was
Born to each Pandava, Dharma, Bhima. (33)

Vivida, Mainda monkeys who became Nakula, Sahadeva,
Are Nasatya and Dasra named Ashwinis; they
Have Indra's element; Dyava, Pruthivi, Rubhu,
Vishwaksena, Uma's son Ganapati and Kubera are inferior
To Mitra-named Surya. (34)

Agni's first son, Pavaka; Chavana, Uchithya sages;
Chakshusama, Raivata, Shwaropita, Uttama named
Rushis, Bramha, Rudra, Indra, Deva, Dharma,
Daksha named seven Manus; Shashibindu,
Pruthu, Priyavrata, Mandhata, Gaya, Karuttha,
Dushyanta's son Bharata; Vrushabha King's son
Bharata; deer-born Bharata, Brahmin-born
Bharata - all have Hari-Vayu element; Shambhu,
Bali, Vidruva, Rutadhama named Indra
Are 8 Gandharvas. (35 and 36)

Kings who are action-patrons are inferior to
Agni by 100 qualities; Bali and other Indras;
Pavaka, Uchitthya are less a little than Ganapati;
Mesha-king, Parjanya became Sharabha named monkey;
Vivaswan Surya's wife Sanjna, Rohini, Shyamala

Are Devaki's incarnations; Devaki, Dharma's wife,
Devaki, Varunapati Ganga Aniruddha patni, Usha are
Six and Agni's son Pavaka are inferior by 2 qualities;
Swaha is lower than Parajanya and six others;
Ashwinis' wife Usha is inferior to Swaha by 10 qualities. (37 and 38)

By Sudarshana disc and Indra's element in Budha
Made him Abhimanyu; Shalya's and Jarasandha's
Daughters are Usha's incarnations; Usha is inferior
To Budha; Shani is lower still; action-patron
Pushkara is lower than Shani; thus opine the wise. (39)

Gandharvas named Tumburu have two incarnations
With Viradha and Udvaha Marut-element; great
Pandit Janamejaya was Chitraratha Gandharva
Born with Trushtra named Surya-element; good
Scholar Damaposhaka and Kadandha named
Demon are Danu-named Gandharva's incarnation;
Swayambhumanu is Bramha-element; Kishore-named
Gandharva as born as Akrura. (40)

Heavenly Gandharva Dhrutarashtra was Vayu-element;
Crocodile that dragged Gajendra and Drupada
Were Ahava-named Marut-element HuHu Gandharva's incarnations;
Virat, with Vayu-element, was HaHa Gandharva incarnation;
Vidyadhara-named Sudarshana was born a
Python that swallowed Nandagapa; Ugrasena
Gandharva was born Ugrasena. (41)

Bramha-element Vishwavasu Gandharva was
Born Yudhamanyu; Surya-element Aryama
Paravasu Gandharva was Uttamajasa; Mitra-named
Surya-element brave Chitrasena Gandharva
Was Satyajit; these have tasted nectar. (42)

Other Gandharvas were born as Bali and
Others and were cow-herds; Pingala, an Apsara,
Shabari and Gopikas were Apsaras. (43)

Agni's sons 16108 became Krishna's wives;
Among them Trushtra' daughter Kasheru
Is senior, in them is Rama's element, she
Has entered them by different names; all
Other Gopikas are equal. (44)

Agni's children Krutu, Sindhu, Shuchi, Pavamana
Kaushika, 100 Gandharvas, Urvashi and other
Apasaras, Menaka, Rushis, Kings are all
Equal to Ajanaja; among them Akhyata
Gods are parents of Anakhyata. (45)

Anakhyatas are inferior to Agni these are
Experts in many arts and everyday worhsip
The best; advise their inferiors. (46)

Among gods there's no Varna-Ashrma; they
Are all equal; Rushis have preceptor-student relation;
Except for 7 ancestors, all others (Chira Pitrus) are inferior
To Ajanajas by 100 qualities. (47)

Heavenly Gandharvas are inferior to Chirapitru;
Earthly Gandharvas are less than Heavenly Gandharvas
by 100 qualities; (48)

Heavenly Gandharvas serve gods; earthly Gandharvas
Are their servants; people who saying; "Shri
Hari is the Creator and promoter of all organs" and
Beseech Him are the best among men. (49)

Vedavyasa, in Bhagawat and other Shastras
Differentiated god-element incarnations;
Though differentiated by 12, 10, 25, 100, 1000
And 10,000 qualities the wise caution no opposition
or conflict. (50)

People, who listen to and repeat god's name and
Story, enjoy doing it expecting no reward, and
Remember Hari who exists in Laxmi, Vayu
And others, and is supreme and worhsip Him

Will be fit for release. (51)

Worldly people have defects; they say "Bramha
And others are Hari's servants; Hari is their
King; Bramha, Vishnu, Maheshwar are equal;
Hari's Avataras suffer from birth, death,
Suffering and fear". (52)

Such people move in bad company, ignorant of
Differentiation; hating the wise they pose as
Sadhus, follow wicked actions and worship
Worthless gods. (53)

I have searched in the ocean of Madhva-philosophy
divine-diamonds,
Strung them in the thread of Kannada,
Made it good, fit for Hari-Vayu. Not finding
Defects the wise should read it everyday. (54)

Incomparable Shri Vishnu, Laxmi, Bramha, Saraswati,
Vayu-Bharati, Garuda Shesha Rudra, Krishna's 6 queens,
Parvati-Sauparni-Varuni, Indra-Manmath,
Ahankarika Prana, Brahaspati, Pravah, Surya,
Varuna, Narada, Agni-Saptarushis, Mitra named Surya,
Ganesh, Pruthu and other Kings, Shani,
Pushkara-Ajanaja, Chirapitrus, Heavenly
Gandharvas, Earthly Gandharvas, Emperors,
Good, middle (moderate), wicked men, among the three
Kinds the earthly Gandharvas, earthly emperors
Best of men, "middle level' men, these four kinds
Of men are eligible for release", I salute them. (55 and 56)

Merciful Lord, existing in Vayu, Laxmi's consort,
Jagannath Vitthal, will grant His presence
According to their ability; those who worship
With devotion, knowing Hari's supremacy and
The differentiation, will be blessed. (57)

Canto XXII

KINDNESS EVEN TO THE SINFUL

(This canto is called "Sakala Durita Niwarana Sandhi". Even though sometimes a devotee makes a mistake or commits a sin, the merciful Lord will, instead of punishing, grants salvation. Sins are pardoned because of previous devotion and present repentance.

The theme appears to be favourite with Jagannath Dasa either because of his personal experience of arrogance and later repentance or because of knowing several instances of redemption. In this canto he illustrates his statements with many examples of how the Lord came to help His devotees in their worst predicaments.)

I have seen not a merciful god equal to Laxmi's consort;
Sudam's beaten rice brought him wealth;
When Draupadi prayed she got many clothes;
Merciful god broke a pillar to save Pralhada. (1)

Devasharma, a Brahmin, out of desperation
Shouted for the Lord's help and Hari
Ran to save him; ignorant people aspire for
Pleasure without worshipping such kind Lord. (2)

I haven't seen in the whole world any one
As merciful as Srinivasa; let Pandits find
In Shruti-Purana; Drona, Bhishma, Krupa
Though in Kaurav army were Pardoned and granted salvation. (3)

The powerful Shri Hari gave Tondaman King conch and disc;
He was pleased with the earthen ornaments offered by potter Bhima;
Most famous, holder of mace and lotus, whose
Head was broken, who on Sita's advice
Married King Akasha's daughter. (4)

He protected Indra when he eloped with Gautama's wife;
Made four parts of the sin of killing demon Vritra;
Bali who stole golden crown of Indra was His
Devotee and Hari became his gate-keeper. (5)

Defectless Hari was pleased with Nanda Gokul
Women despite adultery; though Bramha's father
Was born Nanda Gopa's son and killed demons;
Though Garuda-rider He sat on Gopalas' shoulders. (6)

Worshipped by Laxmi though Hari loved Gopis
(cowherdesses);
Praised by Indra though he herded cows and calves.
Rejected Duryodhana's invitation to accept Vidura's;
Devotee-lover He worked as Pandava's servant. (7)

Protector of three worlds, auspicious bodied,
Purest, friend of gods was Yashoda's son;
With Gopika women's prayer He became their husband,
Lifted a mountain; terror to enemies married Agni's
daughters.[1] (8)

(Note No.[1] : This refers to the many women imprisoned by Narakasura. They were believed to have been Agni's daughters. After killing Narakasura Krishna released and at their request married them even though they were in Narakasura's palace.)

Devoid of form, name, though, He was christened
Krishna by Gargacharya; omnipresent He
Appeared by each form individually; in Dwapara-end
To kill demons was born in Shwetadwipa and saved His
people. (9)

Revered by Laxmi, Bramha, Hari took many Avataras
Protected gods, kings, sages, men; ever-joyful-formed
Lord grants blessings to devotees; granted Sugriva
And Dhruva prosperity here and release. (10)

Killer of wicked demons, mine of excellent qualities,
Grantor of devotees' wishes, remover of worldly illnesses;
Free from fear and sorrow; the cause of creation,
Protection and destruction; joy-incarnate; residing

In every heart, Shri Hari is pleased if remembered. (11)
Ocean of mercy; undisturbed; successful; Laxmi's consort;
Hari frightened Bramha in Bramha-age deluge;
Pleased with Rudra granted him Shesha's position;
Gods who worshipped Him were given nectar. (12)

Mover according His free Will; Master of Himself;
Residing in all things enjoyable and enjoyers;
Himself offering food pleases the patron-gods;
Such a Lord punishes the proud demons. (13)

He the kind-hearted Lord will stretch His protecting
hand the time
His devotees say "Hari Vitthal, protect me"; let
Them say in tiredness, professionally filling up belly,
In severe illness, out of fun. (14)

Anyone who in this world narrates His pleasant stories,
In any form or fashion, will obtain Hari's merciful protection,
Like He did to Sugriva-monkey. (15)

Laxmi's consort, existing in beings, as Shruti
Says "Janatotha Vishnu" (Vishnu who is born),
Is born as per our actions; He indeed is free from birth;
He makes us call and blesses us. (16)

Chief of gods Hari is in humans and called "Nrushatu";
In organs as "Hota", makes each organ work
To obtain happiness; in Vedas as "Rutusatu"
He pleases devotees always. (17)

Bramha's father in water, land and mountains
Is as "Abjagoja", "Adrija"' in pure water,
Sea water, in nectar, lotus, in moon He exists as "Abja";
Sugarcane, Plantains, creepers, grass, bush He is as "Goja";
In mountains is "Adrija"; existing in animate
And inanimate beings He creates diamonds and
Precious things and wild animals. (18)

Veda promoter Shri Hari is omnipresent and

Is called "Shuchi Shatu"; He purifies animate-inanimate
beings;
Incomparable, myriad formed Hari is "Achyuta"
And lives in bodies and acts like common humans. (19)

In guest as food, in Vayu as breath, in
Every mind as thoughtful, acting in world
As knowledge, working time to time as joy;
Living beings are with wife and children to obtain
happiness. (20)

How can such a multiformed Lord appear defective?
Let Brahmin scholars decide impartially;
The moment Hari having a host of names is remembered,
All sins are destroyed. (21)

In land as "Kustha", in ten directions as "Ashastha",
In sky as "Kastha", in each one in each form as "Vyastha",
In all as "Samasta", staying close as "Upastha",
He in the world is "Vishobhana". (22)

In Shastras as "Jnanada", in clothes as "Manada",
In charitable disposition "Vadanya"; Garuda-rider
Acts according to place, being and nature. (23)

Among village seniors as "Agrani", among villagers as
"Gramini",
In villages and small towns as "Shriman"; Laxmi's
Consort as "Yogakshema" protects; which other
Gods have such great story? (24)

Worship Parthasarathi, idol of Garuda-flag;
Whose lotus-feet are worshipped by Rudra;
Grantor of great prosperity; world-enchanting
Beauty; such Shri Hari is always pleased to grant
happiness. (25)

Before creation, gods and living beings are ignorant
Of their work, don't expect it; don't experience;
Then Laxmi's husband creates them to enjoy

Their merit and sin. (26)

Worldly life is painful like sunshine mixed with shade;
Pleasure is fleeting like enjoying obtaining loan;
Shun the wicked; seek the company of
Hari-devotees and obtain eternal bliss. (27)

Worldly life is always like walking in the
Sun with shade; happiness and sorrow, an
Adjunct of past actions ("Prarabdha") will
Never abandon wherever one is; so accept
Shri Hari's "prasada" and "flowers" (worn by idol);
Making friends with the wise, shake off worldly
sorrows. (28)

Cutting paddy, pounding to make rice, cooking
Offering to the Lord, to Brahmins and eating will
Make Vitthal pound all sins; failing this
If eaten sans offering to Hari, will reserve a place
in hell. (29)

Not idling give up worldly pleasures; devotedly
Stand at the great Shesha-sleeper's door; bow down
Saying, "Oh merciful, a doctor to worldly illness,
Cure me"; He will appear before you. (30)

I fail to describe how merciful is Hari! Devotees
Committing heinous crimes are still saved'
Murderer hunter gained supreme knowledge
By Rama's grace and wrote His story. (31)

Ignorant people always beg for something or other;
Lord, make me ask, not even in dream, worldly pleasures;
Make me, life after life, enjoy your devotees'
Company. (32)

Will the wise ever ask for worldly pleasures
When they know that Shri Hari Himself is four-fold worldly
pleasure incarnate,
Four-formed [1] god; ignorant people believing

In worldly pleasures as eternal worship
Ganapati and other gods. (32)

(Note [1]: Four-formed god is Hari in whom are Aniruddha, Pradyumna, Sankarshana, Vasudeva.)

Hari is worshipped by Bramha and others;
Resides in heart-caves of all beings
Is honourable grantor of all desires;
Omniscient; He lives in all, makes them
Act and grants merit and sins suitably. (33)

He does not even once, about anyone,
Shows jealousy, hatred, enmity; "Sudharma"
Named Hari protects every day; incomprehensible
Even to Vedas Jagannath Vitthal grants
Solace to each one to suit his actions. (35)

Canto XXIII

ORDER OF DIFFERENTIATION

(Suprasensory Knowledge)

(Jagannath Dasa's most favourite topic is Madhva Siddhanta. *Harikatha* is written basically to extol Hari or Paramatma and to focus on the Lord's supremacy. As a corollary to it is Madhvacharya's famous theory of differentiation. A few cantos have been written on it and the present one is another to briefly restate it.

In the present canto Jagannath Dasa mentions the differentiation right from Shri Hari to the wicked Kali, and points out the suprasensory knowledge (Aparoksha Jnana). It is therefore called "Aproksha Taratamya Sandhi".

Condemning the crookedminded statements
Of the 21-Schools of thoughts Guru Madhva
Established the Supremacy of Shri Hari; he
Has placed in his heart Laxmi Pati, worshipped well
By Garuda-Shesha; let the Prince of teachers
Have mercy on me. (1)

From Bramha to defectless beings and their
Penances, the time the mortal body disintegrates,
Are what I have told as pushed into my mind;
Let the wise ignoring defects accept the poem. (2)

Grass-eaters, insects, birds, beasts, the best of men,
Kings, Gandharvas, are elementless (divine-element)
Action-obliged good; worshipping Lord's idol
Reflected from body, offer all sense-organ actions
To Hari and are egoless. (3)

The above beings are innumerable; gods are limited;
The uncountable beings are humans, Brahmins,
Having abandoned actions understand Guru's
Words, do work related to occasions and dedicated

everything to Hari. (4)

The above after suffering several births due to wickedness
Are finally born human; relising Hari's supremacy
Offer everything to Hari with wise devotion;
For ten births they worship supreme Hari
Worshipped by gods, as incomprehensible activity maker,
Sorrowless, myriad formed, eternal, creator-protector-destroyer,
Conqueror of birth and death.
For three births more than love for body, house, cattle, wealth, wife,
Friends, sons, mother, father, they work as wanted by
Laxmi's Consort, give up their birth-form and
Visualise Hari in their heart. (5, 6 and 7)

Heavenly Gandharvas, Ajanaja, ChirPitru, are
Wise Yogis; Pushkara, Shani, Usha, Swaha,
Budha, Sanakas, Parjanya have divine-element. (8)

Bearing 100 births in Bharat, being rewardless,
Performing good deeds and then born 1000 times
Achieving the best knowledge; then they in
Three hundred births worship Hari's idol. (9)

Before penance they enjoy no supersensory knowledge;
(Aparoksha Jnana)
They have no prohibited work, no hell;
Settling contradictory statements of Vedas
They establish Hari's supremacy. (10)

From Bramha to Shatastha all from the beginning are devoted;
Among them with superior knowledge and devotion
Bramha-Vayu, Saraswati, Bharati are superior. (11)

Rujuganasthas are naturally devoted;
Gradually they grew; till they reach Bramha-position
Idol-worship increases every age; they are
Sinless, free of three qualities; but Garuda,
Shesha, Rudra and Indra suffer the three qualities. (12)

Before penance Rujugana are ordinary future-observers;
After penance according to abilities they
Visualise actual form of Hari. (13)

Garuda, Shesha and other gods are interrupted devotees;
Bramha-Vayu, Saraswati, Bharati are uninterrupted devotees;
The four work as god's organisers. (14)

Merit and sins are caused to perform by
Vayu; belief in this brings beings closer
To Vayu and avoid low birth;
He despatches to hell people who arrogate to themselves all their actions. (15)

He (Vayu) is in one form in gods, Rushis,
Pitru, Kings and Men and makes them
Do their work suitably; in another form
He becomes a tortoise to bear the world on his back. (16)

Vayu by his third form is hidden in
All beings of 14 worlds, performs 21600 breath-prayers
In sleep, dream and woken stage and makes
Beings do them and undergo sufferings. (17)

Though existing in pure body Vayu has no
Physical binding; he is like burnt cloth;
He is a Siddha Sadhaka; hence defectless;
Garuda-Shesha-Rudra are his servants. (18)

Vayu is one among Rujugana; becomes
Kalki after 100 Kalpa[1] penance; in 99th
Kalpa he is Hanuman then Bhima to destroy
Demons; in Kaliage he is Madhvacharya. (19)

(Note[1] : Kalpa is one day of Bramha or 1000 yugas being a period of 432 million years of mortals.)

Vayu is like Hari in form and with Bramha-
Saraswati-Bharati is in Vedas; with unbroken
Devotion he declares Hari's eternity. (20)

Bearing 3 crore forms in moving animals of sky,

Land, water he kills demons and protects the good.
He is Hari's doorkeeper to Garuda Shesha Rudra. (21)
Each among the Rujus practises penance for 100 Kalpas
And lives in each Kalpa with excellent, auspicious names;
If the wise worship the Lord their great sins
Will be washed and Hari will be pleased. (22)

Lord, Saraswati's husband, favourite of Brahmins,
World teacher I salute you, protect me please;
You have 100 names which are Kalki,
Suteja, Dasa, Dharma, Adharma, Khandana, Varchswi,.
Khashana, Sadhu, Mahipati, Saddharmajana, Dharmaj,
Sampurna, Shuchi, Vaikru, Anjana, Sarshapa, Kharpata,
Shruddhavha, Sandhyana, Vijnana, MahaVijnana,
Kirtana, Sankirna, Katthana, Buddhi, Jaya, Mahattara,
Suvirya, Medhavi, Vijaya, Jaya, Manu, Moda, Pramoda,
Santa, Ananda, Santushta, Charvanga, Charusabahu,
Charu Pada, Sulochana, Saraswata, Suvira, Kapi,
Lampata, Sarvajna, Sarvanjan, Papa Vinashaka,
Dharma Vinita, Sharada, Voja, Sutapsvi, Tejasvi,
Danashila, Yajna, Sutarka, Sushila, Yajvi,
Yagavartaka, Prana, Amarushi, Upadeshta, Taraka,
Kalakridana, Sakarta, Sukalajna, Kala Suchaka,
Kali Samharta, Kali, Kala, Shyamareta, Sadarata,
Subala, Saho, Sadakavi, Gamya, Sujnana, Dashakala,
Shrotavya, Sukirtavya, Mantravya, Kavya,
Drushtavya, Sakhya, Santavya, Kravya,
Smartavya, Sevya, Sabhavya, Svargavya, Bhavya,
Jnatavya, Vaktavya, Gavya, Latavya, Vayu,
Bramha. (23 to 29)

(The above stanzas are a jumble of names. The stanzas are written in the fashion of VishnuSahasra Nama.)

The utterance of auspicious 100 names of the great mentioned
In Vamana Purana grants solace to devotees
In the three worlds. (30)

Hari granted Vayu happiness for 100 births, ruling
the world with ease;
What surprise, the generous grantor of prosperity
To Sudama for a handful for beaten rice, made

Vayu chief of the world. (31)

He will reside in gods under control,
Makes them do penance and he is called Vayu
For 200 Kalpas; having destroyed Daitya
Kali Guru Vayu reaches Bramha-position with wife. (32)

Vayu living among gods for 99 Kalpas is
Called Jivottama; after he is Bramha in middle
Of 100 Kalpa for 87&½ hears he practises
Penances praising Hari. (33)

Only one defect among Rujuganas; they aren't eager
to praise Hari;
Otherwise they would be equal to Bramha; knowledge
And devotion increase to Bramha position; they
Realise first idol-formed Lord then visual presence. (34)

To say Bramha-Vayu suffer from ignorance and fear
Is to fool demons; can never expect lust, ignorance
Fear and sorrow for them; may have pretended
For Srinivasa's favour; it is like the sun roaming
As seen by defective eye or for one suffering from
biliousness. (35)

With pure devotion, knowledge and renunciation
Bramha is always the best; no equal to or better than him;
Having learned Hari's qualities from Rama he can
See Him clearly. (36)

Meditate on Vayu thinking him to possess knowledge-
devotion,
All other qualities of Bramha; the defect in Rujugana
Will gradually be made up; Bharati-Saraswati have
Equal knowledge-devotion; because of position Saraswati is
superior. (37)

Like everything unclear if there is lamp in place of Sun,
Bramha-Vayu Saraswati-Bharati till total release
Find Hari's presence blurred; in deluge, with

God's grace they are not touched by ignorance. (38)

After 100 years in his Kalpa Bramha takes all
Eligibles to Hari's kingdom, makes them bathe in
Viraja river and the kind one enters along with them
Hari's belly. (39)

Defectless released souls after entering Vasudeva's
Belly, come out, obtain Hari's permission move
Around emancipated in Anantasana, Shweta island
And Moksha (salvation). (40)

Bramha, master of Satyaloka, with body full of
Good qualities, has middle and bad qualities in
Atomic proportion; it is for Hari's favour that he
Practises penances for a Kalpa. (41)

For 75 years being Vayu's disciple for Shri Hari,
The practising penance in Lavana sea for
10 Kalpas Mahadeva in 40th Kalpa reaches
Shesha's position along with Parvati. (42)

Indra, accepting advice as Sunanda for 10
Practising penance for Mukunda's "Aparoksha",
For 4 Manvantara, suffers smoke for a crore years;
The Purandar reaches Indra's position and
Enjoys to receive final release. (43)

Sun and Moon were by name Sukhurupa and Shanta
Received advice for 2 Manwantara; practised
Penance of Hari for one Kalpa, stood upside down
For 10000 years to suffer; now they saw Hari's presence. (44)

Rudra-Indra practised penance for many Kalpas
And having Visualised Shri Hari are released
5 headed Rudra did for 50 Kalpas; Indra 20;
Three-sense-patron Ahankar Prana 18; Bruhaspati
Swayambhuva Manu 16; Pravaha Vayu 12; Sun, Moon,
Yama 10; Mitra-Tara 9; Shesha Shastha 8;
Sukracharya, Sanaka 7; Ganga, Parjanya upto

Pushkara 6; action-patron gods 5; Ajanaja 4;
Gopika Women 3&1/2; ancestors 3; Heavenly and earthly
Gandharvas 2; the best of men 1; other small
Beings 1/2; with such penance they will see
God's presence. (45.46, 47)

(The reader will certainly notice here again a good deal of repetition, summarising and unpoetic expressions that, indeed, stop the ethereal flow of *Harikatha*. Jagannath Dasa may not have imposed such indifferent writing on the reader. The poem has fallen into the hands of an inferior poetaster who must have pushed everything of his into the great book.)

Like the lamp-size that drives out darkness
Paramatma exists in Bramha and others
Makes them function to their actions. (48)

Vayu-Rudra, Indra and others in His belly
Assume bodies and serve Hari; ocean of knowledge,
Merciful Lord removes devotees's body and
Mental illnesses, ignores their sins. (49)

He enjoys, in each Kalpa, His creation-protection-destruction;
Swallows Bramha-Vayu like food;
Rudra becomes ghee, other gods are vegetables;
For Laxmi's consort food is three worlds; He Himself is guest. (50)

Like the child in womb eating pregnant woman's food,
Paramatma eats Himself and makes others eat;
Can atom-like feeble being digest such food?
Only ignorant fools would say "yes", not the wise. (51)

He will not be slim with fasting, not be strong after eating;
Incomparable; birthless; incomprehensibly famous;
Devotee-favoured Hari will grant happiness and birthless-ness. (52)

Like sowing in a field, watering and growing
Then himself harvesting, Hari undertakes all
Activities of the world, its birth, protection and death;
Yet is untouched by either happiness or sorrow. (53)

Vayu Rudra Indra and others experience hunger and thirst,
They are for enjoyment; for demons, Preta, Pishacha
They work as obstacle; men animals have
Them and later satisfy them. (54)

Vasudeva is free from sleep, thirst, hunger, fear,
Sorrow, lust, fatigue, forgetfulness, jealousy, merit-sin,
And all defects; So, Bramha Rudra and others
Worship Him and obtain release. (55)

The smallest time-unit is a moment; 5 make a Truti;
50 Truti one lava; 2 lava a minute; 8 minutes a matra;
2 matras make a Guru; 10 Guru a Prana;
6 Prana a Pala; 60 Pala a Ghatika; 30 Ghatikas one
day or night;
60 Ghatikas make a full day. (56)

45 days is a Paksha; 2 Paksha 1 Masa; 2 Masa a Rutu;
3 Rutu one Ayana; 2 Ayana one Abda; 5 Abda a year;
Kruta, Traita, Dwapara and Kali Yugas
Are god's 12000 years. (57)

Kruta Yuga is 4800 years, 3700 is Traita,
2400 Dwapara, 1200 Kali Yuga. (58)

(Human Years) Kruta Yuga has 1828000 years,
Traita 1296000, Dwapara 864000, Kali Yuga
Has 438000 years. (59)

43000 years together make 4 Yugas;
Bramha experiences one day (half day) with
Human years of 43200,00,000. (60)

From human calculation one full day for
Bramha is 864,00,00,000 years; such 30
Days a month; 12 months a year; 100 years
Will see world's creation, protection, destruction and deluge;
This is Bramha's life-span but a moment for
Achyuta; thus say Shruti Smruti; Can Bramha
equal Him? (61)

Birthless, growthless, deathless Madhav experiences
Bramha Kalpa as a moment; RugVeda, Purana
Say that this is just nothing; Laxmi, Bramha, Indra
Obtain His blessings and enjoy happiness. (62)

Can ignorant fools, world-pleasure-involved,
Fickleminded, despicable people enjoy this *Harikatha* drink?
Merciful Jagannath Vitthal will be pleased
If one reads this giving up worldly talks. (63)

Canto XXIV

FORM AND SUPRASENSORY KNOWLEDGE

(Some publishers have called this "Bimbo-pasana Sandhi". Paramatma is the original, beings are His reflections. In every creation of His one sees Hari's reflection. Jagannath Dasa has narrated how Hari's form is seen in His creations.)

For the released Turiya named God-form;
For Bimba Aparoksha He is Vishwa;
For the worldly He is Jaijanana; for the birthless He is Prajna;
Though self-powerful He, being systematic, expressess
Happiness and sorrow till the Kalpa-end. (1)

Annada-named Hari as Prajna exists in Prakruti in cognito;
In Bramha and others Annada-named is bright
Annada-lotus-king (Laxmi's Consort) as Universal,
Has a number of names; knowledge-repository
Hari enjoys Himself. (2)

Annada-named is like ash-covered fire;
In Bramha-Rudra He is Annada; Vishnu-formed
Annada He makes beings happy; who can
Describe such an incomprehensible person? (3)

He is Nada-rupa (sound-form) in the eating sound;
In food and water as one form;
While arguing as voice-form; in belly-fire as peaceful;
In Musical sound of Veda study; as Atishanta
Among sons, brothers, servants; worship such Hari's lotus-feet. (4)

Veda-patron Rama could not serve Him; He is
Ocean of qualities, sans human qualities;
Has placed the entire world in His belly; such
Strange Hari, in wise-accepted Nishusida

Ganapati Shruti, is praised for limitless qualities. (5)

Mayapati Vasudeva grants His Darshana to the released;
Being in great tenets He created in the world
Humans' voice, word, touch, 11 sense organs and five
elements. (6)

In beings' bodies He resides as Purusha along
With Shri-Bhu-Durga and gives hope, avarice,
Ignorance, pride, envy, low lust, hunger, humour,
Happiness, sleep, dream, thirst, wakefulness,
Birth, life, death, merit-sin, defeat victory. (7)

Three-qualified beings are wrapped up in bodies,
And dropped to float in action-full flow;
He makes them world infatuated; those who
Listen to and read (His story) are released. (8)

Believe in Shri Hari who lives in all living humans
And worship; please the good and the bad;
The remover of pain exists in inanimate things
As Anashana; when worshipped thus He will reveal
His real form. (9)

One can meditate on Him in another way;
I shall narrate how the Omnipresent Lord can
Be praised; I am telling this by the grace of
Guru and as my mind thinks; like reflections
Everywhere in a glass-house, the simple-minded
Hari appears in animate-inanimate world. (10)

In satva, rajas and tamas-distributed beings
He is in Vishva, Taijapa and Prajna forms;
In Dareshana, Putreshana, Vitteshana He is
Atma, Antaratma, Paramatma; knowledge-incarnate,
Turya-named Vasudeva is glorious and
Grants release. (11)

Bramha-father resides in animate-inanimate
And makes them act; Kshama, Kshama,

Samihana-named Hari exists;
In ordinary demons'worship and makes them offer Him as "Asham";
Common people offer him as "Mama". (12)

The whole world is Hari's home; though the
Working world is destroyed the creator-Prakuti is permanent;
She is life-less form to Hari; Shri Hari
Resides in Shaligram which doesn't diminish. (13)

One and the only one Lord lives in all beings
Without their knowledge, infatuates them by
Making each one do action; in body He is called
Mute, deaf, blind; how can I extol Laxmi-consort's greatness? (14)

Friend of all, master of world, sorrowless,
Destroyer of devotees' sorrow, worshipped by Laxmi
Hari resides everywhere unconcerned.
Most merciful, protector of good, is praised by Rudra;
He accepts all actions offered by devotees. (15)

Body, house, children, wife, wealth, iron, wood,
Money as good as stone and earth, all have been granted by Hari;
Thinking thus not trapped by false love worship Him everyday. (16)

To Laxmi-Consort all beings are moving forms;
He exists in all and works; in all organs
He, "Hota-named", enjoys everything; makes
Others enjoy and lives fearlessly like a lamp in a windless place. (17)

Like a possessed speaking too much, the world
Functions as if possessed by a huge ghost of Vishnu;
This is true; Sheshasleeper is considered
Different from gods, Gandharvas, Pitru Manav,
Danav-Assembly. (18)

Anantasana, Vaikuntha, Shwetadvipa, the three parts,
Are outside and one inside the world;
The wise consider Him to have four elements[1] or parts;
Realise His four parts and meditate on
Krishna, Uddhava's dear friend. (19)

(Note [1] : Four elements or parts refer to "Chatushpat". He protects beings in four places. His four forms have to be remembered.)

A bent bamboo [1] rides a man's shoulder;
A straight tied with a rope helps an acrobat to climb it;
A Pandit not being reverential to Hari's
Will get tied by Hari. (20)

(Note [1] : A bent bamboo is good for palanquin handle. It therefore is placed on the palanquin-bearer's shoulder. But two straight bamboos are useful to tie a rope on which an acrobat performs his tricks.)

Bright-hued Lord has forms as
Ahita, Vigraha, Sanketika; metal idol
(form) Shaligram, mountains, seven metals,
Boldness, bravery, generosity, cleverness, speech,
Honour, Reverence, pardon, good behaviour,
Holy country, Brahmins, five elements,
Mind and ten organs are Hari's favourite places. (21)

A master of Veda scholars, beautiful-formed,
Lover of music, Lord of gods, pure in work,
Resort to the intelligent; He is nectar-like, eternal
An atom among the inanimate and named
Ajit and Anant. (22)

Money though earned irregularly for Hari's work
Is considered good; money earned meritoriously
But spent for worldly needs will lead to rebirth. (23)

Free and most handsome Hari resides in everyone like them;
Manmatha's father, bright like a crore suns though
Was black like a common man in Krishna incarnation;
Fooling people He enjoys and makes others enjoy. (24)

Like trees and roots growing naturally in a
Forest used as medicines, He will run to you
If you shout "Master of three worlds, protect me." (25)

Shri Hari looks upon His devotees as relatives,
Grants them their desires and stays with them untiringly;
He will accept what is given; ask nothing
Worship Him and freely wander like a proud elephant. (26)

To gods He fulfils their wishes with no asking;
To humans only when asked; to demons He
Grants not though beseeching anxiously;
Fools perform daily rituals, enjoy worldly joys and visit hell. (27)

Like Sun spreading his rays to form shadows of things
According to size, Disc-bearer Sankarshana
Is shadow of animate-inanimate world and
Sunshine, too, to suit their abilities. (28)

Thus Hari with Laxmi, Shridevi, Bhudevi,
Extends his aura everywhere; devotee-patron,
Externally merciful, lotus-eyed, Maya's consort,
Accepts worship but residing in all gods
Shows Himself as a servant. (29)

Om-promoter, Veda-patron, best, strange,
Ever-auspicious-qualitied, incomparable,
Served by all, ocean of qualities, unconquerable,
Myriad-formed, Hari is pleased with those
Who worship not expecting anything; He is
Unperturbed and non-visible. (30)

Like a lamp showing Shri Hari in the darkness of world,
A terrace to a mansion of all pleasures is
This *Harikathamruta*. Jagannath Vitthal
Lifts from the sorrowful world those who
Drink the nectar of *Harikatha*. (31)

Canto XXV

RISING DIFFERENTIATION

(The canto narrates differentiation from the inanimate to human emperors.)

Shandilyarushi, listening to devotees' prayers
Narrated differentiation among released and non-released.
Among non-moving, plant-life is better; insects are
Better than plant-life; goat, sheep, cow, elephant,
Tiger and lion are better than insects; better
Than them are good-actioned shudras; Vaishyas,
Then Kshatriyas; better than these are Brahmins;
Scholarly Brahmins are better than ritual-doing ones;
Emperors are better than them. (1)

Earthly Gandharvas are better than emperors;
Heavenly Gandharvas are superior; Rushis
Numbering 9999990900 are better than heavenly Gandharvas;
Apsaras (Krishna's wife) are their equals;
Better than them are Chira Pitru. (2)

90 Rushis, 100 Tumburu, Urvashi and other
100 Apsaras, and Ajanajas are better than
Chirapitru; 16000 rushis, sons of Agni,
Are slightly inferior to them; among them
Kasheru is superior, equal to her are
24 Ajanajas. (3)

(Again a good deal of repetition. The earlier remarks made hold good here.)

Gopika women are equal to Agni's 16000 Rushis;
Pushkar is better than them; Shani better than Pushkar;
Agni's wife Usha better than Shani; Budha than
Usha; Swaha better than Budha. (4)

Anakhyatas, famous among gods, are better than Swaha;
Than Parjanya; Aniruddha's wife Usha, Ganga.

Sanjna, Shyamala, Rohini are senior to Parjanya;
Karmaja gods are better than them. (5)

Pruthu, Nahusha, Shashibindu, Priyavrata,
Parikshit are senior to Bhagirathi; Bali
And other seven Indras, 8 Pitrus, 8 Apsaras,
11 Manus, Shukracharya, Uchithyas, are
Equal to Karmaja gods. (6)

Kubera, Vishwaksena, Ganapati, Ashwini are
Equal to 85 Shesha Shatasthas; Surya,
Preceptor's wife Tara, Dikpalakas, Pravahas,
Are better than 85 Shatasthas.
Great Rushis Marichi, Pulastya, Pulaha, Krutu,
Vasishta, Angiras, all Shri Hari's divinity in Bramha,
Are equal to Vishwamitra, Vaivaswata Muni;
Agni, Bhrugu, Daksha's wife Prasuti are
Senior to Mitra. (7 and 8)

Narada is better than Agni; Varuna is
Better by 1/4 qualities; Yama, Moon, Sun,
Shatarupas, are senior to Varuna; Pravaha Maruta
Is senior to all; better than him are
Aniruddha, Bruhaspati, Swayambhu Manu, Daksha,
Shachi. (9)

Ahankarika Prana is better than the six;
Kama and Indra are senior to him;
Gauri, Varuna, Sauparni are better than them;
Krishna's 6 queens are better and Jambuvati
Among them having Rama's divinity is superior. (10)

Garuda, Shesha, Rudra are better than Krishna's queens;
Better are Saraswati, Bharati; better than them are Bramha-Vayu;
Rama is superior to them, none equal to her. (11)

How can I extol the greatness of Laxmi, Mukunda's wife?
Causes creation, protection and deluge through
Bramha-Rudra-Indra and gets them their positions;

Deathless Laxmi meditates on Achyuta saying;
"Universal Lord, my Lord." (12)

Such great Laxmi can never equal an iota
Of myriads of unlimited qualities of Hari;
Lives in His heart conquering space and time;
Can there be a computation of Hari's qualities and extent?
(13)

Bramha-Rudra and all beings occupy a part
Of a hair in a body of one form; seven
Islands, seven seas, Meru-Mandara mountains
Palaces of Bramha and 7 protectors of world
Are all merged in it. (14)

Shri Hari is supreme in all countries;
Omnipresent; complete in all qualities;
Ever free in manipulation; all-support;
Present in all; facing all; all-named;
Revered by all; Eternal; wish-fulfilling
All desires, conquering all; and for all. (15)

People who write the ascending differentiation,
Who learn it, will have their desires realised;
Hari, present in all gods, ocean of mercy,
Grantor of release, devoid of fear, sorrow,
Will remove all sins and bless. (16)

For those desiring Hari's lotus-feet-sight that grants wishes of devotees,
The differentiation from inanimate to Bramha-world
Is a ladder; it will dry up worldly ocean of
People who remember mentally, by speech and body.
It will lead to knowledge, devotion, renunciation and
prosperity. (17)

Fragrance of sandalwood and others are different when
offered to fire in sacrifice;
Likewise three-quality-surpassed, famous, remover of sorrows,
Shri Hari differentiates the merit-sins of gods, and humans.
(18)

Jagannath Vitthal is devotee-favourite, fortune-creator,
Alone, Universe-supporter, Supreme, free of defects,
Impenetrable, incomprehensible, self-luminous,
Powerful, Eternal, all-Veda-mentioned, honourable,
Honoured, Laxmi's consort, minute and huge. (19)

Canto XXVI

DESCENDING DIFFERENTIATION

(In this canto Jagannath Dasa narrates the differentiation or ranking right from Shri Narayana to man. He points out very cearly that the narration has been gift of Gurus and the Lord Himself.)

I narrate in brief by my Guru's grace
Differentiation of Laxmi's Consort's devotees
Starting from Bramha and other gods.
I salute Keshav, Narayana, Laxmi, Bramha-
Vayu, Saraswati-Bharati, Garuda-Shesha,
Krishna's six queens, Sauparna-Varuni-
Parvati and Indra. Let them give me wisdom. (1)

I salute Hanuman; Aniruddha, Manu, Guru,
Daksha, Shachi, Rati, Pravaha Vayu, Sun, Moon,
Yama Shatarupa, Varuna, Narada I salute
And beg for a path of renunciation. (2)

I bow down to Fire, Bhrugu rushi, Prasuti,
Seven sages, who are Bramha's sons, and Vaivaswata Manu,
Vishwamitra,
Demon Niruruti, Tara, Pravahi; I always salute
Ashwini, Ganapati, Vishwaksena. (3)

Leaving 85 Ukta Sheshasthas, I salute Manus,
Uchithya, Chavan, Yamala, Kartaviryarjuna and
100 action (Karmaja) gods, rain, Ganga, Sanjnya,
Rohini, Shyamala, Usha. (4)

Agni's wife Swaha, Moon's son Budha, Ashwini's
Wife Usha; Shani, I salute always. Everyday beings'
Action-patron is Pushkara; him I salute. (5)

I salute Ajnaja, 16000 Agni's sons, Gopikas

Who joined Krishna, ancestors, 100 crore rushis,
Heavenly singers and worldly singers, emperors;
I bow down to the devotees of Rama's Consort. (6)

Those who pray according to this rank
Will obtain religious and other desires fulfilled.
Forget not to worship humbly the master of all
Jagannath Vitthal. (7)

Canto XXVII

ORDER OF SALUTATION

(Jagannath Dasa has extensively discussed Madhva Siddhanta's principles of differentiation (Taratamya) in cantos 20, 21 and 25. However, since every Madhva considers it important, Jagannath Dasa reiterates it in the 26th Canto. This canto is short and is quick to finish reading for a worldly-busy man. He felt that the matter should be condensed still further and undertook to summarise it in only 5 stanzas. His main desire is that Hari's devotees should learn the five stanzas by heart and repeat them everyday. The same principle of differentiation, being very vital, is repeated 6th time in the 29th Canto. It is named "Anu Taratamya" (brief differentiation.)

The wise may please listen, I have narrated
The order (of salutation or Taratamya) from the
Best of men to Sankarshana.
I salute followers of Madhvacharya's principles,
The wise, the best of men to action-patron gods;
I bow down to Uktasheshasthas, deities,
Parvati, Sauparni Varuni, Krishna's six queens,
Rudra, Saraswati Bharati, Vayu, Bramha, Laxmi and
Narayana. (1)

The prosperous Bramha Vayu is eclipsed by
The rich Laxmi Narayana; He grants good wishes,
Soft, residing in three worlds, having three strides,
Pure-famed, charming, loved by Bhudevi, beyond
Three qualities, Guru of all, Samasong-lover, is
Jagannath Dasa's personal god. (2)

Demon-destroyer Rama saved Gajendra;
Not visible to mind and word; grantor of mental happiness;
Bearing an excellent qualities; King; bestower
Of release from world and place in heaven;
He is pure; wish-fulfilling tree to devotees. (3)

Hari has golden hue; independent, Omnipresent;
Eternal; sleeping on Shesha; beyond Varna [1] and Ashrama;
Promoter of Vedas; Garuda-rider; mine of
Great qualities. (4)

(Note [1] : Varnas are four, Brahmana, Kshatriya, Vaishya and Shudra. Ashramas are Bramhacharya, Gruhastha, Vanaprastha, Sanyasa.)

He is a repository of innumerable qualities;
An indistinguishable forms incarnate; eternal,
Different from animate-inanimate; Lord of
Three worlds, Jagannath Vitthal will ever remain with His
worshippers. (5)

Canto XXVIII

IN PRAISE OF GANAPATI

(Praise of Ganapati should have come in the beginning itself. But what prompted the Dasa to place it as the 28th Canto, almost at the end of the book, is beyond comprehension. Is it any interpolator's work? One does not know it.

Ganapati's blessings are badly needed to do any work successfully. He is obstacle-remover and has the right of priority. The Dasa's Guru Gopala Dasa, it is believed, was an incarnation of a part of Ganapati or Vighnaharta. Perhaps Jagannath Dasa, out of respect for his Guru and life-giver, has written a special canto in praise of Ganapati.)

Also, there is a legend often narrated about the present canto. Ganapati who volunteered to write the Mahabharata was blessed by Vedavyasa for his meritorious work. The blessing was, "No work be started without Ganapati's prayers. No writing without his praise would be completed." Ganapati, it was said, was very angry because Jagannath Dasa had not remembered Him even at the end of the work. After the 27th Canto Jagannath Dasa, despite God's grace, could not proceed with his work. The hands would not move, mind refused to function and the poem was almost sabotaged. What had happened to the *Harikatha*? Jagannath Dasa could find no answer. Jagannath Dasa was dumb-founded and did not know what to do. Meditating on Laxmi Narasimha, his favourite deity, he spent the night restlessly. In his dream that day he saw Ganapati. He told the Dasa that because Jagannath Dasa did not praise Ganapati the work could progress no more. Immediatley Ganapati disappeared. The Dasa woke up with a shock and found total darkness. But early next day he started, with no problems, writing Ganapati's praise. It worked smoothly and turned out to be a beautiful composition. Other writing too, proceeded quickly. This legend may appear to be far-fetched. But it is not only very interesting but expresses Ganapati's greatness and generosity in pardoning the Dasa for the remiss.)

Son of Rudra, who is like a honey-bee at Hari's lotus-feet,
Ganapati shine everyday in my mind. Vedavyasa's
Favourite, sky-patron, kind god save the good.

I beseech you to lift me from the problems. (1)

I pray that you kindly watch me. One-tusked,
Elephant-faced, bedecked in gold ornaments,
Vighnaraja, grant your company to the good that
praise you. (2)

Ganapati, fix my polluted mind on Hari's lotus-feet.
I am not afraid of hell or fire, remove my sins and
protect me. (3)

You are equal to Kubera; Vishwaksena; god's doctor,
Ashwini;
Shanmukha's brother, greater than Sheshashatastha,
Honoured by Ganga, universally praised Lord, I
Beg of you with pure mind to grant me devotion and
understanding of Hari. (4)

Born to Krishna-Rukmini as Charudeshta;
With Rudra's blessings, Krishna's orders, you
Punished arrogant demons to relieve world's miseries,
Merciful Lord I salute you, grant me knowledge. (5)

Shining with elephant ear, who humbled Moon,
Bright like rising sun, who tied a snake around belly,
Strange in appearance, bearing weapons, who
Destroyed the wicked, Ganapati, you are witness
To all actions; generous god, protect the good. (6)

Sky-patron, with devotion wrote Vyasa's books,
Understood them with ease, made them famous.
Weapon-bearer, I bow down to you, Make me
Understand those books.

You reside in Hari's lotus-navel; look beautiful
With red colour; pure god in the world; friend of other gods;
Made a mouse your vehicle; have the capacity of Vayu;
Named Prabhu, grant wishes of devotees. (8)

Rudra's son, granting worldly pleasures to demons

Who practised "Sankata Chaturdashi" ritual
In your name you fooled them; I salute
You every day; show me Krishna, disc-bearer. (9)

Worshipped by Siddhas and Vidyadharas,
God of fulfilment, bless me to have knowledge,
Intellect, pure devotion to Hari; make me
Rmember Him always. (10)

Wearing two red shining clothes, great Bhagawat,
Magnificent-bodied god, listen to my plea.
Grant me strength to abandon worldly pleasures and to fix
My mind on Bhagawat philosophy. Great scholar,
Save me from fear of worldly existence. (11)

Indra worshipped you to kill demons; great warrior
Rama worshipped you before building the sea-bridge;
On Krishna's advice, Dharma worshipped you;
Vakratunda, how fortunate you are with Lord's grace. (12)

Duryodhana was destroyed with family for
Worshipping you not; Our Guru Bhima destroyed them;
(Madhvacharya's previous incarnation)
Brother of Shanmukha, reside in my body
To lead me to religion. (13)

Fond of 21 sweets (Modaka), making mute speak;
Lord, wishfulfiller, expert in writing, extend
Me your hand to destroy mental sins; born
Of Parvati's body-dust, I pray to you. (14)

Ever auspicious, giver of world's creation-protection-
Destruction-knowledge, mover of god-demons'
Mental activities, hater of bad deeds, devoted
To his worshippers, such a lord meditates on
Hari and grants happiness. (15)

Grant me knowledge of five-element differentiation;
Make me visualise Hari; grantor of wishes,
Lovingly accept a Haridasa like me, as your

Own servant and beguile me not in world.
Rudra's son, prevent my sense organs from
Drawing in wordly ocean. (16)

Great man, I seek nothing from you; not
Afraid of low birth; but grant me wisdom
To know that all actions are done by Hari. (17)

Salute to Guru, conqueror of sleep, wish-fulfilling
Tree of devotees, senior god, mine of good qualities,
Parvati's son, my sense organs are tired of
Worldly ego; remove them. (18)

Victory to Vighneshwara, remover of difficulties,
World-auspicious, grantor of learning, fearless,
Angerless, charming god, look with mercy
To remove worldly pain, illness and death. (19)

I salute your feet you big bellied-god,
You are kind; leave me not but protect me;
Remove obstacles in my good work; repeat
And make repeat Lord Hari's name. (20)

Let Jagannath Vitthal, master of Vayu, accept
Through Parvati's son, this 21 stanza red lotus garland;
May He grant release to His devotees in heaven. (21)

Canto XXIX

DIFFERENTIATION IN BRIEF

(Jagannath Dasa has narrated the differentiation from Paramatma to Kali, The narration briefly covers the different levels.

It may be noted that the theory of differentiation is an important aspect of Madhva philosophy. It proves the unquestioned supremacy of Shri Hari. Out of thirtytwo cantos of Harikatha as many as eight have been directly devoted to the discussion; many other cantos, too, mention the theory very often. Since the theory of differentiation is considered by Jagannath Dasa as a holy scripture, wish-fulfilling, he narrates it elaborately almost to the point of tedious repetition.)

Vishnu is supreme; Laxmi is inferior to Him
By a myriad qualities; Bramha-Vayu are inferior to her;
Saraswati-Bharati are lesser; Garuda-Shesha-Rudra are still less;
Krishna's 6 queens are still inferior; Jambuvati among them is divinity-oriented and is great. (1)

Sauparni-Varuni-Parvati are mutually equal;
But inferior to Jambuvati; Indra-Kama are inferior;
Ahamkarika Prana is inferior to the two; inferior
To him are Aniruddha, Shachi, Rati, Daksha,
Prajapati, Swayambhu Manu; Pravaha Vayu is
Inferior to all the six. (2)

Yama, Surya, Chandra, Shatarupa are mutually equal;
But inferior to PravahaVayu; Varuna is inferior to Surya;
Narada is junior to him; Agni, Prasuti, Bhrugu
Are mutually equal; they are inferior to Narada;
Atri, Vishwamitra, Vaivaswata Muni are inferior to Agni and others. (3)

Mitra-named Sun, Acharya-wife Tara Niruruti,
Pravahi are equal; but inferior to Vishwamitra;

I shall tell about Shatasthas later. (4)

49 Maruts, 2 Ashwini, 10 Vishwadevatas, 11 Rudras,
12 Suns, One Guru, 3 Pitrus, 8 Vasus, one chief
Vayu-Bharati-Pruthvi-Rubhus are eligible to drink Soma. (5)

(Of 100 told) 15 are senior gods, others are equal to Kubera and Ganapati;
Good Vaivaswata Manu, Swayambhu Manu, Tapasa-Manu; all other 11 Manus
Are inferior to Ganapati. (6)

Chavan's son, Shukracharya's brother, Uchithya,
Agni, Dhruva, Nahusha, Shashibindu, Priyavrata,
Pralhad, all kings are inferior to Ukta Sheshastha;
Rohini, Shyamala, Usha, Janhavi, Virata, Parjanya,
Saunjna - all mutually equal but inferior to kings. (7)

Abhimani goddesses are inferior to Ganga;
Narada to Uchithya are inferior to the above;
Swaha is inferior to some Rushis; Budha is
Inferior; Usha is inferior to Budha; Shani is
Lesser than Usha; praised by the good Pushkara is still lower. (8)

8 Rushis are lower than Pushkara; Urvashi and
100 Apsaras, Tumbari and 100 Gandharvas are
Ajanaja; Agni's sons 16100, Krishna's wives are
Equal to Ajanaja. (9)

Unmentioned Apsaras are inferior to the women-companions of Krishna;
Heavenly Gandharvas are superior to human Gandharvas;
Kings are 100 qualities less. (10)

Best of men are lower by 100 qualities than kings;
Remember the gods superior by 100 qualities;
They will grant happiness. (11)

Lesser in quality than man are trees, creeper than tree,

Grass than creeper, bush than grass; rule-controlled
Man is inferior to all; inferior still are
Ignorant beings; bad-natured servants are lower;
Lust-anger-patrons Namuchi and demons are
Lower than them; Viprachitti demon is very low. (12)

Kali's wife Alakshi is worse than Viprachitti;
Kali is the worst; none as bad as him in
Three worlds; the wise remember him while
Urinating and defecating and while walking
In darkness and in dirty roads. (13)

Bramha is patron of the good; Puranjana is
Patron of worldly beings; chief of demons is
Kali; Vayu, to please Hari, exists among
All works and makes them work. (14)

Pranadeva is very powerful among gods, men and demons,
Works suitably and makes them act; grants
Knowledge and devotion to gods, borrow-joy-mixed
Knowledge to the middle (moderates) and ignorance
And infatuation-hatred to demons. (15)

Thus knowing difference between gods and
Demons, realising Laxmi Consort's supremacy
Worship Him; Jagannath Vitthal will be
Pleased and grants blessings. (16)

Canto XXX

DIFFERENTIATION AMONG DEMONS

(Like differentiation among gods, there is ranking among demons. One has to understand the heavenly differentiation to receive Hari's blessings; one has to study differentiation among demons, too, to ward off dangers. One has to be away from the wicked. How can one know the wicked unless he studies them carefully. It is for this reason that Jagannath Dasa has devoted a full canto to discuss the differentiation.)

With respectful devotion Bramha narrated to
Vasudeva, the chief of all, Laxmi's consort, demons'
Nature and qualities.
Bramha said, "I have great devotion for you;
So have Vayu, Hanuma, Bhima, Madhva. Ignorance
Of theirs creates difference. Demons think it so and are
Fit to enter dark hell. No doubt in it. I'll
Slit tongues of those who insult you." (1)

Calling Hari, a mine of knowledge, power, joy,
Qualityless; assuming self as god; alluding
Birth to Sacchidananda; saying that Laxmi and
Hari separate; calling impregnable, unconquerable
Shri Hari to be afraid of weapons are stupid demons. (2)

Demons say that Rama has fear and sorrow
When He really has none; call Parasurama
And Vedavyasa ordinary Brahmin and rushi;
Tell that Rama and Krishna forms have a haircut;
Say that Krishna worshipped Shiva to beget children. (3)

Demons again say that Rama, to wash sin, fixed Shivalinga;
There are differences in the Avatars of Hari;
Holy places alone are sacred; call gods their
Gurus, Parents, King, Idol and kind people. (4)

They are demons who call beautiful and
Self-created images to be Hari's forms; salute
Shivalinga man-fixed; assume Shiva, Sun,
Shri Hari to be one and the same; announce sun to be
The only supreme god are haters of Vishnu. (5)

Placing Shaligram in Ashwattha, Tulsi leaves,
(banyan tree) (basil)
Shivalinga and bowing down to it will
Always grant release; he who expecting earthly joys
Salutes without Shaligram will go to hell. (6)

He indeed is demon who salutes separately
Ignoring Shri Hari; Hari does reside there not;
Believing the existence of Hari in Bramha-others
Will always have His company. (7)

Only shudra will accept Shiva as supreme;
He will worship Shivalinga, Hanuman, Rama-Krishna idols,
Newly planted Tulasi in Vrindavana, uncalved cow,
(basil)
Ashwattha-unmarried[1] ; he indeed is demon; he will always suffer. (8)

(Note[1] : Ashwattha tree is ceremonially married to neem tree. Then only it assumes divinity.)

From Bramha to best of men are eligible for release;
Kali has Bramha's lifespan; from the worst of men
To Alakshi, demons are hatred-infested; still
None equal to Kali in wickedness. (9)

Bramha-life-span-demon is Kali; other demons
Residing in purgatory wait for him; after
Bramha's 100 years Kali's body will be mace-broken
By Vayu and despatched to permanent hell. (10)

Bodiless demons suffer in hell; enemies of
Hari and His devotees suffer more even in hell. (11)

Falsehood is knowledge; unbearable sorrow is
Demons' earned knowledge; Kali, too, has the same suffering;

His wife is inferior to him by 100 evil qualities;
Kalanemi who became Kamsa was 100 less. (12)

Madhu-Kaitabha who were born Hansa, Dibhika
Were 5 qualities[1] less; Ila's son Narakasura was
Equal to Viprachitti; Rudra's devotee Narakasura
Had 100 qualities more than Hiranyakashipu. (13)

(Note[1] : Qualities here mean evil nature, bad qualities, Words inferior and superior have a slightly different meaning in this comtext. Inferior in bad qualities here suggests less of evil nature. Superior suggests more of evil nature.)

Hiranyaksha was 3 qualities less than Hiranyakashipu;
Vanimanta is his equal; Bakasura is less;
By 20 qualities demon-chief Tarakasura was less;
By 6 troublemaker Shambasura is less. (14)

By 6 qualities inferior to Shambara are Hidimba, Banasura,
Dwapara, Kichaka; but equal among themselves;
Dwapara was Shakuni, Duryodhana's uncle. (15)

Namuchi, Ilala, Pakanamed demons are equal;
Namuchi is less by 10 than Bana; Vatapi is
Wicked by 3 qualities; bad-minded Dhenukasura
Is less by 100 than god-enemy. Vatapi; evil Keshi
is ½ less. (16)

Keshi and Nrunavarta are equal; by 11
Lavana is less; Arishta is less by 5 than him;
Demon-chief Hansa, Dibhika, proud Vena,
Poundrika Vasudeva are inferior to Lavana by nine. (17)

Evil-natured Dushyasana who said he was
Himself god, Vrushasena, demon-leader Jarasandha,
Are equal; they are superior in wickedness;
Kansa, Kupa, Vikarna are equal; Rugmi is
By 100 less than them; great demon Shatadhwani
And Kirmiras are equal. (18)

Among drunkard demons Kalikeyas are low; when
They have divine-element they are better than others;

There are patron demons of mouth, hands, feet,
Ears, anus, Vagina, penis, nose, skin, tongue; each
One is less by 100 than the other and less than Kalikeyas.
(19)

Patrons of sense and action organs are Kali and others;
They reside among all and make them commit sins;
Saraswati-Bharati-Bramha-Vayu being uninterrupted
Devotees have no demon-element; this is a test for Hari's
devotees. (20)

Kali's element enters Rudra and others;
Saraswati-Bharati-Vayu and their incarnations
Remain unaffected; Bramha with folded hands
Prayed to Hari. (21)

Believing it to be a sin to narrate demons'
Differentiation, is demon's job; indeed such
Narration is merit-earner; Veda Vyasa in
Garuda Purana suggests grief for such demons. (22)

Thorns, sharp-pointed stones prick bare-feet; will
They bother a shoe-wearer? There's no sin hearing
The killing of snakes and scorpions; men who
Hate demons are not afraid of Yama's people. (23)

Offer your merit-sin to Hari in whom are
Gods from Pushkara to Bramha; He will
Double merit and bless you; sins are multiplied
To give sorrow to Kali and others; Hari, eternal,
Revered, blesses suitably the moderate humans. (24)
(middle-level)
Three-qualitied Shri, Bhu, Durga, Bhargavi's Consort,
Best of gods Jagannath Vitthal resides among
Three-type beings and grants blessings to suit their
actions. (25)

Canto XXXI

OFFERINGS TO THE LORD

(Whatever we eat should first be respectfully offered to god; it is His due; He has created them. This is a religious principle. Though Hari never accepts all food that is offered to Him still He takes whatever essence there is in the offerings. After He "eats", His devotees should partake of the food. Lord is present in whatever things we use. Each thing has one presiding god; we should meditate on the patron gods when we offer food. Ultimately, Vishnu who is present in all deserves every offer. We should remember Him. We should say, "Shri Madhva antargata Shri Krishnaya" (Shri Krishna in Shri Madhva.)

Garuda-rider, ignoring Laxmi begot
Bramha from His navel; obtained gods
From His body; like children protects all;
Sorrowless, joy-incarnate, demon-enemy
Shri Hari protected Arjuna as his charioteer. (1)

He hasn't an iota of defect; has many incarnations;
Does strange actions; extraoridinarily intelligent;
Consort of Maya; residing permanently in
Madhva's inner love (heart); Shesha-sleeper; wearer

Of Kaustubha and other diamonds; repository
Of joy, strength and beauty; how can I narrate
Glories of such Hari. (2)

Shashana and Anasha are Keshava's two forms;
The wise follow Shrutis that say that He
Is in Swarupadeva and Sthuladeva;
They worship Him always and are like fire;
One has to learn it. (3)

Full of good qualities; free from defects of
Birth and death; visible to gods; invisible to humans;

Free of worldly life; enemy of Kamsa; non-familied;
Having many incarnations; promoter; diseaseless;
With many sun-peaceful; most affectionate
Relative; let Him protect me. (4)

Laxmi-consort exists everywhere in animate-inanimate beings;
Wears each person's form, lives incognito, does all
Their work and makes them work. (5)

Fearless, giver of knowledge, Lord of past, present and future,
Demon-enemy, Garuda-rider, Kamala's husband,
Unworried, Vayu's favourite, ancient, Bramha's father,
Loved of the wise, such Shri Hari protect us. (6)

Killer of the wicked, super-famed, praised by Vayu,
Grantor of all desires, self-master, joy-incarnate,
My family deity, ever-pleased, strong, suffering-endurer,
Creator-protector-destroyer, favoured Gajendra,
Such Hari, I salute. (7)

(The reader will notice a series of repetitions stanzas in praise of Hari; either Jagannath Dasa himself, as a ritual repeated them which is not likely, or some hack-writer put them into the beautiful poem. A good-scholar-editor like Jagannath Dasa would have mercilessly chopped off all dross from the grain. *Harikatha* would certainly have gained immensely in poetic qualities if many repetitions are removed.)

Who is worshipped by Indra, flattered by Rudra,
Destroyer of Sita's sorrow, easily pleased, shining
With gold-colour, Laxmi's mind-fixed-on-Him,
Killer of Madhu, One-and-the-Only-one-formed,
Existing in gods, Hari, save us. (8)

Immeasurable, multi-formed, always-smiling-faced,
Grantor of release-joy, whose feet are worshipped by gods,
Self-luminiscent, omnipresent, quick-blesser;
World-Emperor, chief of Yadus, incomprehensible,
And Vishvataija-and-Prajna-formed Hari. (9)

Like blue clouds moving with wind, Bramha-Rudra,
Indra-Surya and other gods and quality-patron Laxmi
More with Paramatma. For all Shri Hari is

The progenitor and grantor of release. (10)

Will a person's efforts to move clouds by fanning succeed?
Shri Hari resides in beings, makes them do
Merit-sins and grants fruits; the wise
Salute Him and cross worldly-ocean. (11)

Destroyer of pain, lust, ignorance; spreads
Like sky in the world; always with a smiling face;
Vairaja- named Hari protects His people without
giving them pain. (12)

Like a looker of his face in a mirror fixed,
The holy people without a mirror see His
Face everywhere and enjoy. (13)

Meditate on Hari in moon food-patron is merciful Keshav;
In Bharati Payasa-patron is Narayana;
In Surya eatables-favourite is Madhava called Hiranyarashmi;
In Rama, Shruti-praised, ghee-patron is Govind. (14)

Meditate on Vishnu in Saraswati milk-favourite;
In "Mandige" (a sweet cake) Bramha-hidden Madhusudan;
In butter Trivikrama in Vayu;
In curd Vamana in Varuna and Moon. (15)

Garuda is soup-patron; in him remember Shridhara;
Mitra-named Surya is in green-vegetable in him is
Hrushikesha;
Shesha is patron of banana and sweets;
In him is Padmanabha; think of Him. (16)

Meditate on brave Damodara who resides in
Gauri, patron of sour eats; meditate on
Sankarshana who resides in Rudra, patron of non-sour eats;
Praise Vasudeva who is honoured by the wise always;
He resides in Indra, patron of sweet things. (17)

Remember Pradyumna in Bruhaspati who exists in food
articles;

Praise Aniruddha in Yama existing in bitter eats;
With devotion pray to Purushottama in Manmatha
Residing in mustard, asafoetida, cardamom and camphor. (18)

Juice sucked by tongue; in milk, in glue-oil-fried
Eatables is Chandra's son, Budha; remember
Adhokshaja who protects him, meditate on
Laxmi-Narasimha in Daksha existing in
Asha-gourd, sesame and "Udida". (19)

Meditate on Achyuta in Manu residing in "Wada"
and other eats;
Praise Janardana in Niruti existing in salt;
Salute Upendra in Prana living in fruit juice;
Meditate happily on Hari in Ganga existing in
betel-leaves. (20)

Veda-patron Hari is in Budha residing in excellent water;
Krishna is in Him; Pushkara, who does
Good actions, purifies all food offered and
Then offer it to Hamsa-named god. (21)

Rati is a patron of all sweet things; remembered
In her Vishwa; remember Parashurama in
Agni; Vasanta in fuel and cow-dung cakes;
In him is Vrushabha who be devotedly prayed. (22)

Remember sorrowless Vishwambara in Mahalaxmi,
Who exists in the cook; remember Varaha
In Bhudevi existing in clean rectangle;
The wise worship Sanatkumara in Ganapati who is food-
cover-patron.(23)

Vishwaksena in Prakara form hides food for Srinivasa;
In him is Purusha-named god to remember;
Shri Hari, worshipped by Guru Vayu,
Is always worshipped and worshipper. (24)

Laxmī is in new, delicious, food fit for
God-offering and always pleases Him;

Worship her who is fearless and is joined
By Jagannath Vitthal. (25)

Canto XXXII

DIVINITY DIFFERENTIATION

(This canto is called "Kaksha Taratamya Sandhi" by some publishers. Even though the subject of differentiation has appeared ten times in *Harikatha* each time it is emphasized. This is the last canto and should have ended with a benedictory note. Jagannath Dasa has followed a different benedictory method in which he has, according to differentiation saluted all right from Shri Hari to the best of men. Since the theory of differentiation is rated very high by Jagannath Dasa he has repeated it here.)

Shri Ramana, chief of all omnipresent, eater of essence,
Free, free of all defects, full of qualities like knowledge-
Power-wealth, devoid of three qualities, mine of qualities,
Many-formed cause of world's creation-protection-destruction,
Merciful, Lord Narasimha protect the good. (1)

Always free, free of passions, always joy incarnate,
Support to real and unreal world, worshipped by
Masses of released and unreleased, listen to my
Pleas, residing in Hari's chest, devotee-dear,
Mother of three worlds, famous Goddess protect us. (12)

Ramadevi visualising countless forms in countless
Hair-cavities, seeing the whole world of universe,
Their form and nature, is every moment
Astounded at her Lord's magnificent form. (3)

Watching in one myriad of forms, in each
Part a countless, in each nail a countless forms,
Thinking with amazement the numberless qualities,
Bramha stood with folded hands and lisping
With emotion accepted defeat in failing to
Describe the Lord. (4)

How fortunate indeed are Bramha-Vayu!
Shri Hari's pure and beautiful form they
Could see and enjoy. Fortunate are they!
Even Rudra could see Him not, what of poor humans? (5)

Bramha worshipped Ramapati for 100 Kalpas,
Pleased Him and became powerful Hanuma-
Bhima-Madhva and was born in
Lord's navel-lotus; I salute Bramha-Vayu. (6)

They see Vasudeva's form like a pole star in
The sky of heart and happily praise Him;
Saraswati-Bharati are they; lovingly I
Salute them and pray for knowledge and devotion. (7)

Garuda carries Him who has put the world
In his belly, Garuda holds His feet, watches
Lovely Krishna-forms in each finger-nail;
Praises Him. May he grant good days to all. (8)

Not reached by Yogis'heart and mind, praised
By Vedas and Puranas such Lord is praised by
Two thousand tongues; Hari has spread to earth,
Sky and netherworld; he, Shesha, provides bed for
Shri Hari's yogic sleep, I salute Shesha. (9)

He, who rides a bull,with Ganga on his head,
Moon on head, auspicious, Tryambaka, Killer of Andhaka,
Wearer of tiger and elephant hide, Bramha's son,
Respected by world, shining like pure crystal, is
Parvati's husband. I salute you. (10)

Ornamented by snake's hood, with matted hair,
Holder of sweet music drum and trident,
Three-eyed with Agni, Surya, Chandra, grantor
Of devotees' wishes, whose lotus-feet are worshipped
By demons, gods and Rushis, who has humbled
Ravana such Shiva always protect me. (11)

You have destroyed Daksha's sacrifice, Virupaksha,

Favourite of renunciation, grant us bliss
And protect; you are Kubera's friend, a
Wish-fulfilling-tree for devotees, enemy of Vrika,
Chief of world, Mahadeva, with Shuka, Durvas,
Jaigishavya incarnations, be pleased with us. (12)

Sitting in Lavana sea for 10- Kalpa-penance you
Pleased Hari; by His orders you spread false
Shastras to fool demons and fix them in
Purgatory; wearer of hides you become eligible
For Shesha position; I salute you. (13)

I salute Krishna's favourite wives Lakshana,
Jambuvanti, Kalindi, Nila, Bhadra, Mitravinda,
All six queens; reside in my heart-sky with
Your husband to protect me. (14)

With Shri Hari's grace you with suprasensory
Knowledge see Lord's forms and listen to
Stories of His greatness; you, Sauparne, Varune,
Parvati I salute; wash my faults and grant
Auspicious days. (15)

I salute Devendra's feet; he, like spring cuckoo,
Sings melodiously the praise of moon-like Hari;
He is in heaven with wish-fulfilling-tree and
Cow and precious diamond Chintamani.(16)

Kruti husband Pradyumna is extraordinarily powerful;
Manmatha in Ketumala island always worships
His loveliness and qualities; I salute Rati-husband
Manmatha; let him remove our mental illness. (17)

I salute as my great teacher Ahankara Prana
Who increases our activities; he worships
Shesha-sleeper Hari who has infinite greatness
And is worshipped by nine-type devotion[1]. (18)

(Note[1] : The nine types of devotion are Shravana, Kirtana, Smarana, Padasevana, Archana, Vandana, Dasya, Sakhyam, Atmanivedanam.)

Rati, Swayambhu Manu, Daksha Prajapati, Brahaspati,
Shachi, Manmath's son Aniruddha who have
Joyfully resorted to Hari as a numberless-branched-tree,
In world bring me auspicious time.(19)

Like a new boat to cross ocean of worldly problems
Is the hearing, singing of Harikatha; Pravaha
Vayu is a boatman who helps cross the ocean;
Let him protect devotees' family. (20)

By his father's orders, to lift common people, he
Begot children as Swayambhu Manu; mother
Shatarupa, I salute you physically and mentally;
Bless us with good days. (21)

Oh, Yama, like 4 Purushartha (Dharma, Artha, Kama,
Moksha)
You bore four children, Nara, Narayana, Hari,
Krishna; you are equal to Surya, Chandra and
Shatarupa; you send the sinful to hell and
Protect me good; kindly support us. (22)

Moon born of Madhusudana's mind, shone
During Amruta Churning residing on Rudra's head;
I worship your lotus-feet every day, like a
Honey-bee; removemental worry. (23)

Let the Sun who residing in lotus-eyed Hari's eyes,
Extending rays as though to handshake, put
Me in the company of the wise day and night. (24)

Repository of qualities, having begotten Laxmi
You wedded her to Shri Hari; so, He lives with you;
Bramha and others always stand to attention;
I cannot praise you; grant me a good mind. (25)

I salute heavenly sage, Narada, who has "tilak" on
his forehead.
With a neck shining with Tulasi necklace,
With rhythmic music on tuned Veena in hands;

He is singing Om-orginator's (Hari) songs and is moving
happily. (26)

The Munis on Saraswati river asked Bhrugu
To visit Bramha, Rudra, Vishnus' world to
Find out each god's great qualities; he stated
Hari as supreme; such Bhrugu grant me all Purusharthas. (27)

I salute Agni's incomparable power; by Hari's
Orders he, a mouth, transports sacrificed things
To each one. Let him grant me knowledge, fame, education
and intelligence. (28)

Equal to Agni is Prasuti; under father's orders
You bore 60 famous girls and married them
To people with honour; I salute you, protect my family. (29)

Bramha's 7 out of nine sons were great
Ascetics; the unconquerable (Hari) induced to favour them
In "Samadhi" (transcendentalism); these Marichi,
Atri, Pulah, Krutu, Vashishta, Pulastya,
Vaivaswata, Vishwamitra and Angiras, I
Salute. (30)

Of 11 Adityas Mitra-named Surya, Pravaha's
Wife Pravahi, Niruruti preceptor's wife, Tara
These everyday remove Adhi, Vyadhi, Upatala,[1]
And grant the wise good times. (31)

(Note [1] : Adhi means mental problems, Vyadhi refers to physical illnesses; Upatala is a collection of mental and physical problems.)

Honourable Vishwaksena, Kubera, Gajanana
And their equal 85 Sheshatastha are saluted
Every day. Let them remove falsehood and
Lovingly grant real knowledge. (32)

BhutaVayu-patron-sage Marichi, Indra's
Son, Jayant patron of feet, favour us;
Let them not involving us in worldly pleasures
Grant us pure knowledge of Hari. (33)

I salute Pralhad who rejected his teachers,
Emphasized Shri Hari's supremacy to all;
When his father insisted on seeing Hari
Pralhad showed a pillar out of which
Appeared human-lion (Narasimha). (34)

From Bali to 7 Indras are action-patrons;
Other 11 Vasus, Auchithya, Chavan and 80 rushis
KartiViryarjuna, Pruthu King who shook the earth,
Angaraka, Parikshit, Nahusha, Nabhiraj, Yayati,
Shashibindu, Priyavrata, Bharata, Mandhat,
And other 100 pious kings; Jaya-Vijaya,
8 Gandharvas, Pavaka, Sanakas, 7 Ancestors,
And Chitraguptas be kind to us. (35 and 36)

Vishwakarma, Urvashi and others enjoying
In pure lakes, Rahu-ketu enemies of
Sun-Moon, Dhumarcheshas who are guides
To Shri Hari's path; all these are equal to
Action-patron gods; let them bless us. (37)

Ganga, Shyamala, Sanjna, Rohini, Cloud-proud Parjanya,
World-patron and Aniruddha's wife Viratadevi,
Agni's wife Swaha - I salute all these, let
Them with no obstacles grant me strength
To worship Hari. (38)

I always salute Budha who appears
Like honey-bee to Bramha's father's lotus-feet,
Clean-water-patron; let him grant us
Prosperity. (39)

I bow down to Yashoda and Devaki
Who saw Lord's child-play and who
Was hugged affectionately; Hari is unreachable
Even to the minds of Laxmi-Bramha;
He has no birth or death. (40)

Let Indra's doctors Ashwinis' wife Usha cure good peoples'
Illnesses and protect them; Indra is

Hari's purifying name-patron. (41)
Oh, mother Earth, Hiranyaksha had
Stolen you but the Lord as Varaha
Brought you up at gods' request;
I salute your feet and request you
To ignore sins of touching you by feet. (42)

She has made oceans her clothes; mountains
are her breasts beautiful; supporter of
Animate-inanimate beings; with perfume
And sandal qualities; daughter of the
Best of Sages, Kashyapa; wife of Varaha;
I salute you respectfully, pardon my defects. (43)

Surya's son, Shani, is punishing
Sinners who worship not Hari; not
Once forgetting I salute you; lift me
Drowning in the worldly-ocean. (44)

Let Guru Pushkara, who, according to
Shri Hari's desire grants results to beings
Who perform good deeds, remove obstacles
In my good work. (45)

I salute Srinivasa's 16100 wives, daughters
Of Agni, 70 Yakshas, 30 demons, and servants;
These are equal to Ajanaja; also I salute
Some Apsaras. (46)

A few Gopikas practised lovingly Katyayani ritual
On Jamuna to marry Krishna;
Some with their body-touch charmed Bramha's father;
These two types of wives. I salute, Let them
Fulfil my desires. (47)

Kinnara, Guhyaka, Rakshasas, Pannaga,
Pitru, Siddha, all are respectable and
Equal to Ajanajas; I salute them to
Grant happiness and fame to devotees;
How can I describe their qualities? (48)

Out of 100 crore sages 100 rushis are
Excluded; I salute all others saying "Save me";
To Bhuripitrus I bow down to grant
Auspicious time. (49)

The most auspicious of the auspicious Rama's
Consort's qualities are sung with ease, concentration,
Sweet voice, in Indra's court by heavenly Gandharvas;
I salute them. (50)

I bow down to earthly Gandharvas who have
Been singing the all-world-famous Laxmi-consort;
Except Pruthu, Bhagiratha kings I salute
Other kings with clear mind. (51)

The best of men enjoy Shri Hari's form in
Their heart; I bow down to them; let them offer
Devotees' desires. (52)

I salute the mass of Vaishnavas who are like
Honey-bees to Hari's lotus-feet; they have spread
The world over and are Madhvacharya's disciples;
Can I mention their names? Let them grant me knowledge
every three hans. (53)

Chief in obtaining Manmath's father's mercy;
Most eligible Bramha, Saraswati, Rudra, Indra
And others' differentiation-narration is
Read by devotees, Rama's consort will grant all desires. (54)

If this is read three times one's mind, body
And speech will improve; all sins will be removed every day;
Fear of thieves, fear of kings, fear of aquatic animals
Like crocodile, fear of sharp weapons, water,
Fire, ghost, serpent, fever, hell will never occur. (55)

Victory to the person strange among three worlds;
The only cause of world's creation; Janaki's consort;
Conqueror of old age and death; Ganga's father;

Destroyer of demon family; remover of worldly
Illnesses, Jagannath Vitthal, victory to you;
May you always protect me.

Shri Krishnarpanamastu
Finished on Thursday, 10 January 1991.

Canto XXXIII

BENEDICTORY CANTO

(This canto is called "Falastuti Sandhi" and, as already mentioned in the introductory note, is written, not by Jagannath Dasa, but by his best disciple. Karajagi Dasappa or ShriDa Vitthal has written this. As a disciple who has read the poem with intelligence, appreciation and admiration, Shri Da Vitthal has written about *Harikatha*.)

Harikathamrutasara as recited by Guru-chief
Jagannath Dasa in all cantos looks clear
Like a fruit in the palm; the Pandits not
Themselves reading it ask others to read;
To them it burns like fire; such Pandits
Should read it not or teach it not. (1)

Written in Bhamini Shatpadi this poem
(apoetical form of 6 lines)
Tells about Hari's greatness, the differentiation,
Right from the first canto; those who read this
Every hour get Sudama's friend, Krishna's
Hand to cross the worldly ocean. How can I
Extol His mercy? (2)

What is essence? The answer is *Harikathamrutasara*;
Our teacher has stated Parthasarathi's acceptable
Ways; One who follows the right path told here
Has no worldly existence. (3)

Hari, pleased with our great Dasa,
When he longed to sing Ramesha's praise,
Sat on his tongue and narrated it;
In this meritorious poem no effort was
Made for rhyme or metre; critics praise it;

Hari-haters may make a wry face; they deserve
Not the nectar of the poem. (4)

Haters criticise this as written in Prakrut; (Kannada)
Will the good reject it? With Hari's
Qualities pure in the poem Prakrut itself,
Becomes Sanskrit; what wonder is there? (5)

If not auspicious to ear, incomprehensible to dullards,
Not acceptable by Shruti-Smruti, the poem be rejected;
Our Guru has, as though churned the milk-ocean
Of Madhva's writings to take out essence, and
Made *Harikathamrutasara*; Bramha-knowledge-seekers
Accept it; non-Vishnu devotees need touch it not. (6)

I am not flattering the poem though defective because of my devotion to my teacher;
The poem contains no repetition, dry figures of speech,
Play on words, expressions unacceptable to rules,
Irrelevant, declensions; or how will the Lord receive the composition? (7)

Jagannath Dasa is a wish-fulling tree to instant-poets,
The whole country knows him (I need not tell);
I salute all Hari's devotees and repeat it; this poem,
Harikathamrutasara, should not be recited to
Haters of Hari; thus do I beseech. (8)

Not struggling for rhyme, nor searching puns,
Not placing the short for the long vowel, nor stepping
The smooth flow of Shatpadi (metre); accepting
The hateful comments as ornaments *Harikatha*
Is composed with knowledge realised by the intelligent. (9)

Unheard of idea, deeper meanings will be known
By some effort; then the magical book makes people
Forget themselves in a bath of joyful tears; the common
Worldly beings will enjoy half the beauty; demons
Not obtaining joy will have sorrow like cutting their body with weapons;

The true devotees will never miss the Siddhanta in this. (10)
Really, true devotees who will appreciate the poem and follow
It will increase their mental purity; even the
Ignorant will benefit by listening to it; one who
With knowledge tries to block impurity sincerely
Will indeed be blessed by Paramatma; what surprise is
there in it? (11)

This poem will be honoured in wise company; will
Pour philosophical-tenets; seeds of lust-anger are
Destroyed; false knowledge closed; those not accepting
Differentiation should lose their teeth; Jagannath Dasa
Has shown the path for Hari's devotees to forget themselves,
By diving deep into the knowledge of Hari. (12)

Is it Vyasatirtha's favour, master Vitthal-worshipper
Purandara's kindness on him (Jagannath Dasa) I can't
comprehend?
He wrote Harikatha offering a garland of
Keshav's qualities to Shri Hari almost equal to the work
of Vadiraja. (13)

Harikathamrutasara, full of nine qualities (Rasas),
Very magnificent, like an ocean, enjoyable and
Vastly ornamented; son of Narasimhacharya,
(Jagannath Dasa)
Has done a great favour to good men never to be
forgotten. (14)

Can an ordinary man on earth drink celestial nectar
And digest it? He will be considered a Pandit;
He will prove himself a food if he vomits it.
Auspicious to the ear *Harikatha* will be appreciated
By those whose mind is fixed on Hari; only the
Deserving like it, not the undeserving. (15)

One who reads even a word in this poem with love,
Will not be rejected by gods; giving up four-fold
Desires (Dharma, Artha etc) and concerntrating devotedly
On god makes him a free man; for him is *Harikatha*

Not for others. (16)
One who reads *Harikatha* has always good fortune;
On-coming obstacles are stopped untimely death
Halts putting fear in the heart of Yama's servants,
All desires are achieved and the Lord dances
In such a house. (17)

Even if a good man reads one canto of *Harikatha*
He will enjoy in plenty long illness-free life, prosperity, fame,
Strength, bravery, generosity, good magnanimous
Qualities. (18)

Blind man will get back sight, deaf can hear,
Non-growing mind and body will have Manmath's
Qualities if he just listens to the poem;
Sterile animals bear calves, dry wood sprouts if
One even pretendingly reads *Harikatha*. (19)

Merit is gathered due to bathing in holy waters,
Performing rituals and abstaining from avarice, more
merit is obtained.
In knowing each stanza of *Harikatha*; therefore
One should recite *Harikatha* loudly for the devotees
To nod their head in appreciation. (20)

Husband's service for wife, devotion for wife
In husbands will joyfully occur; they will
Be happy, follow teachers and eleders and
Reach auspicious time in the world. By
Reading *Harikatha* they will attain salvation. (21)

How can I describe? I fail to comprehend
Everything; in what way can I narrate
Bhagavanta's myriad qualities? One who
Has written a poem explaining Madhvacharya's
Tenets with suitable examples is Jagannath Dasa.
He who considers him to be a common
Human will go to hell. (22)

In diamond-studded plate most delicious food

Served first to Krishna is graciously accepted;
Likewise to the learned is offered *Harikathamrutasara* in golden-Kannada plate
Counched in excellent words;
The author has generously poured Lord's knowledge
in their ear. (23)

Those who read *Harikatha* everyday with devotion will be
Accepted by Krishna by His extended hand
As His disciples; He minds not whether they
Are wicked, fattened by vices, fallen due to
Evil deeds. Thus speaks Shri Da Vitthal. (24)